D1061658

THE
FIVE RINGS
MIYAMOTO MUSASHI'S
ART OF STRATEGY

THE
FIVE RINGS

MIYAMOTO MUSASHI'S
ART OF STRATEGY

THE NEW ILLUSTRATED EDITION
OF THE JAPANESE WARRIOR CLASSIC

TRANSLATED BY DAVID K. GROFF

CHARTWELL
BOOKS

This edition published in 2016 by Chartwell Books,
an imprint of The Quarto Group
142 West 36th Street, 4th Floor
New York, NY 10018 USA
www.QuartoKnows.com

For R. L. K.

The Five Rings
Translated by David K. Groff

Managing Editor: Christopher Westhorp
Managing Designer: Suzanne Tuhrim
Picture Research: Julia Brown and Emma Copestake
Production: Uzma Taj
Commissioned calligraphy: Yukki Yaura
Commissioned map artwork: Robert Nelmes

ISBN: 978-0-7858-3400-7

7 9 10 8 6

Typeset in Adobe Garamaond Pro and Lorrenne
Printed in China

Notes:
Abbreviations used throughout this book:
CE Common Era (the equivalent of AD)
BCE Before the Common Era (the equivalent of BC)

This edition is published with the permission of and by arrangement with Watkins Media Ltd

Captions for preliminary pages
Page 1: A 19th-century colored woodcut depicting Miyamoto Musashi
with two *bokken*, or wooden quarterstaves.
Page 2: A man in traditional samurai costume at the Sanja Matsuri, a festival held each year
at the Asakusa shrine in Tokyo to honor the *bodhisattva* Kannon.
Pages 4–5: Mist shrouds the sacred Kii mountains in Honshū's modern-day Nara prefecture,
the historical Yamato province.

Contents

Miyamoto Musashi: his life, his writings and his legacy

Miyamoto Musashi is known in Japan as a *kensei* 剣聖, a "sword saint" – a title reserved for those who go so deeply in perfecting the art of swordsmanship that they achieve a deep spiritual enlightenment through it. Given Musashi's presence in Japanese culture – he is depicted in everything from novels to video games – it is perhaps surprising that so little is verifiably known about this legendary figure. Soon after his death, popular accounts began to circulate among storytellers and kabuki dramatists, and the elements of his life quickly became embellished to the point that it was difficult to disentangle fact from fiction. What is at all reliably known comes mainly from a few letters, some family records and two histories written almost a century after his death: the *Bushū Denraiki*, written by a former vassal of the Kuroda clan, with which Musashi had been associated during the earlier portion of his life, and the *Bukōden*, written by a retainer of the Hosokawa clan, in whose hospitality Musashi spent his last years.[1] However, through these and his own writing, an outline of Musashi's life can be developed.

JAPAN IN MUSASHI'S TIME

During Musashi's lifetime, his country underwent the transition from the incessant fighting of the Sengoku 戦国 ("Warring States") period, encompassing the Muromachi and Azuchi–Momoyama periods (1336–1573 and 1568–1603, respectively), and ushered in, with the early Edo period, what would become more than two centuries of relative peace and stability under the Tokugawa shogunate.

Prior to that, the last strong central government had been the Kamakura *bakufu* 幕府 ("tent government") military dictatorship; it had lasted from its foundation in 1192, by the shogun Minamoto no Yoritomo, until 1467, when social and economic strife culminated in the Ōnin War and the downfall of the Minamoto clan's Ashikaga shogunate. This marked the beginning of almost 150 years of various clans vying for power, including the Takeda, Imakawa, Hōjō (which had ruled for many years under the Kamakura *bakufu*), Hosokawa, Miyoshi and Oda clans, among others.

The last of these produced Oda Nobunaga, whose ruthlessness might have enabled him to unify Japan, had he not been betrayed and taken his own life in 1582. The void left by Nobunaga's death was filled by Toyotomi Hideyoshi, who in 1590 reunified Japan and brought the warring *daimyō* 大名 clan leaders to heel, following the siege of Odawara, near what is now Tokyo. However, due to his lack of Minamoto lineage, Hideyoshi – a former footsoldier – was unable officially to take the title of shogun; his lack of a successor and a failed invasion of Korea left his influence weakened, and not long after his death Tokugawa Ieyasu, an old ally of Oda Nobunaga's, seized power when his eastern-raised forces defeated the Toyotomi supporters of the western-raised army at the Battle of Sekigahara, in 1600.

After this pivotal battle, Tokugawa control of Japan was essentially complete, and remained so until the late 1800s and the Meiji restoration. The Tokugawa shogunate was headquartered in Edo, and the 250-odd years that this period lasted saw an unprecedented prosperity and stability, and the rise of a large, urban, middle class.

The way of a warrior

This peace had other ramifications, one of which was a huge shift in the function of the samurai class. While *samurai* 侍 literally means "one who serves", in the sense of a retainer to a feudal lord, for hundreds of years the title had also been associated with the *bushi* 武士, a hereditary class of warriors – and that connotation persists to this day. During the years after the fall of the Kamakura *bakufu*, the *bushi* were constantly in demand due to the conflicts between warring *daimyō*. However, with the taming of the *daimyō*, the samurai were gradually reduced mainly to the status of local bureaucrats, although they retained the trappings of warriorhood (including the wearing of two swords, a privilege which was not allowed to commoners, and a shaved top of the head).

While the *bushi* had always stressed the need for a balance of scholarly, cultural education alongside the military requirements of their profession, with the transition to the Edo period the samurai became increasingly occupied with these more leisurely pursuits. Musashi clearly found some of these developments distressing, and his opinions to that effect are reflected in his comments in the *Go Rin no Sho*.

Musashi was of the "old guard": it is telling that he refers only to *bushi* and *buke* 武家 ("war houses" – that is, warrior clans) in his texts, never using the term samurai.

Schools of swordsmanship

The life of a warrior in Musashi's time was one of constant training and proving oneself. Swordsmen often engaged in a period of *musashugyō* 武者修行 or "warrior austerities", during which they would submit themselves to monk-like conditions as they travelled from place to place looking for adversaries against whom to test and polish their skills. If they were fortunate enough to survive and make a name for themselves, swordsmen might obtain a position of service to a *daimyō*, but then too they had to be ready if called upon to fight. Even in pitched battle, single combat was often the rule, and samurai would frequently announce their name, lineage, and sometimes school of swordsmanship in "calling out" their opponents on the field.

By the 1600s many schools had developed, all in competition for prestige and students, as well as contracts, to train the *daimyō* and their retainers. The schools' styles were extremely various, with myriad specialized postures, sword-grips, styles of footwork and other movements as their "trademarks". Some of these techniques were thought to allow faster or more powerful strikes; others were ways to distract or confuse the opponent. Schools also specialized in particular weapons as a way of identifying themselves, with exceptionally long or short swords, or weapons of surprise

such as the sword-cane; some made their names by codifying
a multitude of techniques for a panoply of weapons. Musashi,
however, saw this all as being not only mainly decorative
("a lot of flowers but not much fruit") but essentially
irrelevant to – and distracting from – the true work of striking
the opponent down, not only physically but also spiritually.

At the same time, the era was also one of cultural
advancement. Sen no Rikyū largely formalized what is now
known as the tea ceremony; the itinerant Zen priest Takuan
Sōhō wrote some of his classic texts in this period (fictional
accounts, notably Yoshikawa Eiji's *Musashi*, have Takuan
connected directly with Musashi, but there is no evidence
that the two ever actually met); and the sword-polisher and
man of culture Hon-ami Koetsu was leading the "Kyōto
Renaissance", bringing together men of genius from all
realms and all walks of life. It was into this vigorously
changing world that Miyamoto Musashi arrived.

THE LIFE OF MIYAMOTO MUSASHI

Shinmen Musashi no Kami Fujiwara no Genshin,[2] as he calls
himself in the *Go Rin no Sho*, better known as Miyamoto
Musashi, is believed to have been born in or around 1584 in
the village of Miyamoto-Sanomo (hence his being known as
"Miyamoto" Musashi), in what is now Okayama prefecture,
although Musashi himself claims to hail from Harima,
present-day Hyōgo prefecture.[3] As a boy and a young man
he was known as Bennosuke. His father was almost certainly
Hirata Munisai, a respected expert in the martial arts,

especially that of the *jitte*.[4] The Hirata family were vassals of
the Shinmen, retainers of the Tokugawa clan, which rose to
power during Musashi's lifetime. Some stories relate that the
young Bennosuke was trained in the martial arts by his father
before they parted ways, when Munisai divorced Musashi's
mother while the boy was still young. Later, Musashi was
taken in by an uncle and educated at a Buddhist temple.

A combative boyhood
In 1596, at the age of twelve or thirteen and big for his age,
Bennosuke fought Arima Kihei of the *Shintō* Style, as noted
in the *Go Rin no Sho* (see page 44). Accounts of the fight have
the young Bennosuke hurling his opponent – an arrogant
swordsman of little actual skill – to the ground and beating
him to death. Some time later, possibly when he was about
fifteen, Musashi left Miyamoto and travelled to Tajima (in
present-day Hyōgo), where he had a duel with a martial artist
of some renown by the name of Akiyama, an episode which
Musashi also mentions in the scroll "Ground" (see page 44).

 If Musashi participated in the Battle of Sekigahara
(1600), as is sometimes claimed, he would have been around
sixteen. However, it is extremely difficult to place Musashi at
this decisive event in Japanese history. It is not certain where
Musashi was at this time, but he may very well have been in
northern Kyūshū, serving with the Kuroda clan, whose
members were supporters of the Tokugawa; this whereabouts
would be in direct contradiction to popular accounts that
put him on the losing side of the conflict at Sekigahara.

According to the *Bushū Denraiki*, Musashi at this time was indeed in Kyūshū, where, reunited with his father Munisai, he fought for the Kuroda in the siege of Tomiku Castle.

Acquiring a reputation and developing a style

It is generally agreed that in 1604, when he was about twenty, Musashi fought his famous bouts with the Yoshioka brothers, who were well-known in the Kyoto area as instructors of swordsmanship and ran a respected *dōjō*[5] (school of martial arts) in the city. Musashi defeated each brother in duels, ruining their reputation. After this, he may have gone on to the Hōzōin Temple in Nara to have bouts with the teachers and students of a style of spear-fighting developed there.

By now Musashi was teaching a martial arts style he called the *Enmei* ("Circle of Brightness") *Ryū*[6], as is evidenced by certificates he issued around this time. Sometime between the ages of twenty-one and twenty-three he also wrote out the style's precepts in a text called the *Hyōdōkyō* 兵道鏡 ("Mirror to the Way of Strategy"). It specifically describes the use of the *jitte*, suggesting that this style may largely have been based on teachings from his father, who was a recognized expert in that weapon. The text also explains the use of two swords, indicating that this was a practice Musashi had been employing since early in his career and not, as some have suggested, something he developed later.

Musashi then went to Edo (today known as Tōkyō), on the way encountering and engaging in combat with one Shishido Baiken, a warrior famous for his skill with the *kusari-gama*, or chain-and-sickle. It is recorded in one account that Musashi mimicked Baiken's swinging of the chain over his head by swinging his own short sword round and round similarly, then hurling it, hitting Baiken in the chest and killing him. That the *Enmei Ryū* contained techniques for the *shuriken* 手裏剣 (throwing-knife) lends some degree of credence to this story. Once in Edo, Musashi also took on members of the *Yagyū Shinkage Ryū* ("New Shadow Style") school (whose Yagyū family founders were teachers to the shogun), defeating them as well. He met Musō Gonnosuke, a renowned practitioner of the staff, and engaged in bouts with him at least once. Gonnosuke was unharmed, and by some accounts even fought Musashi to a draw; in any case he went on to found the *Shindō Muso Ryū* ("God-Way Dream Vision Style") school of staff-fighting, in which he included techniques to be used against two swords.

After staying in Edo for a few years, Musashi returned briefly to Kyōto. There he practised Zen meditation at Myōshinji, a temple of the Rinzai Zen sect, which focuses its practice on the use of *kōan* 公案 – the Zen conundrums.[7] According to the records of the Hosokawa clan, at Myōshinji he met Nagaoka Sado, a retainer of Hosokawa Tadaoki, one of the great *daimyō* of Kyūshū, and predecessor of Hosokawa Tadatoshi, who would provide Musashi with patronage in his later years. According to the *Bukōden*, Nagaoka told Musashi of a talented warrior named Sasaki ("*Ganryū*") Kojirō, also known as the "Demon of the Western Provinces", and suggested a match for the two. Whether Musashi did in fact meet Nagaoka at Myōshinji or not, there is wide agreement that it was through a connection with the Hosokawa clan that he came to have the most famous bout of his career.

The birth of a legend

Musashi was twenty-eight years old in 1612 and had already made a name for himself – both as a warrior to be reckoned with, and as a carelessly dressed iconoclast who used strange tactics that derived from no specific tradition and often wielded for weapons whatever happened to be lying around. Sasaki Kojirō was practically a polar opposite: carefully groomed in the Toda school of swordmanship, fastidious in dress and manner, and famous for his use of a sword of such great length it was known as the "Drying Pole". Kojirō had mastered such elaborate techniques as the *mizukuruma* ("waterwheel") and *tsubame-gaeshi* ("swallow-turn"),[8] and had founded his own style known as the *Gan-Ryū* ("Massive-Rock Style"). Under the auspices of the Hosokawa clan, it was arranged for the two men to meet in single combat on a small island known as Funashima (which translates as "boat island"), off the coast of northern Kyūshū, near Kokura.

Accounts of the bout differ: Musashi overslept and arrived late; Musashi was early and waiting. Musashi was chased after the match by Kojirō's seconds; Musashi left Kojirō alive, but he was finished off by Musashi's followers. All accounts have the following in common, though: Musashi arrived in a small boat and waded to shore with a makeshift *bokutō* wooden sword fashioned out of an oar.

An angered Kojirō (possibly due to Musashi's lateness, or to his attitude, dress, and choice of weapon) drew his long blade and threw the scabbard into the waves. At this Musashi declared, "Who throws away his scabbard except someone who knows he will have no need of it later?" This further enraged Kojirō, who quickly attacked. Although the knot in Musashi's headband was nicked by Kojirō's long blade, he dodged the blow and met the attack with one of his own, striking Kojirō in the head and making him fall. From the ground Kojirō struck out at Musashi, but only managed to cut his *karusan*[9] trousers. Musashi then struck again, ending the bout – Sasaki Kojirō either died on the spot or shortly after; Musashi quickly boarded his small boat and departed. The island became known as Ganryu-jima, or Ganryu Island, in memory of Musashi's fallen opponent.

This was the match that made Musashi's legend, yet strangely enough Musashi never refers to it in writing. The bout was pivotal, in that it brought Musashi greater fame and respect among the powerful Hosokawa clan, but perhaps more importantly it may have been the turning point in his approach to the martial Way. Musashi writes in the *Go Rin no Sho*: "… sometime after I turned thirty, I thought back over my past, I realized that I had not won all those bouts because I had achieved great levels of strategic skill. It could have been because I had some innate gift for this path, and thus did not get away from its natural principles, or because those other styles of swordsmanship were lacking in some respect" (in "Ground", see pages 44–45). It is possible that

Musashi had met a very worthy opponent in Kojirō, and maybe had his first really close call, making him realize that he was, at this point at least, not actually invincible, and causing him to begin his quest for "the deeper principles".

An itinerant servant

In 1614 the forces of Tokugawa Ieyasu were trying to complete the consolidation of power that had begun with their victory at Sekigahara. At the heart of this campaign was the siege of Osaka Castle. From the winter of 1614 to the summer of 1615 bloody battles raged through two sieges there, and Musashi was in the fray (most likely, given his status thereafter, he was on the victorious Tokugawa side). According to the *Bushū Denraiki*, during these engagements Musashi killed great numbers of the enemy with a *naginata* passed down from his ancestors, adding expertise with this weapon to the many already known to be in his arsenal.

After Osaka, Musashi was employed by the powerful *daimyō* Ogasawara Tadazane, returning to Harima to teach swordsmanship (as well as the *shuriken*) at Akashi Castle, which he also had a hand in designing and building. Now in his early thirties, Musashi's battlefield experience had given him first-hand understanding of the virtues and weaknesses of the various features of fortifications, but Ogasawara apparently saw a broader talent and engaged Musashi to assist in the planning of the town, and also of some gardens. Here we see evidence of the familiarity with "all the arts" that Musashi would later write about.

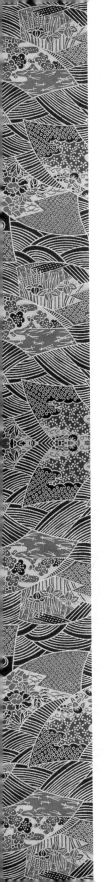

Musashi had by now established himself as a talented and valuable asset, and it seems he never wanted for money or employment. Although he never sought an official post, which may have implied too many restrictions for one so resolute about his freedom, when Musashi was in his mid-thirties he went to Himeji to work for the *daimyō* Honda Tadatoki, taking with him a recently adopted son, Mikinosuke. Musashi played a part in the layout of this town as well, in addition to more gardens. While he was there he also taught swordsmanship; news of his presence spread quickly, which led to another match that Musashi makes no mention of – against Miyake Gunbei of the *Togun Ryū*, reputed to be the best swordsman among Honda Tadatoki's vassals. Possibly encouraged by Honda himself to test Musashi, Gunbei petitioned for a match, but was quickly beaten. Musashi spared him serious injury, though, and this control so impressed Gunbei that he asked Musashi to take him on as a student of the *Enmei Ryū*. In fact, after his encounter with Sasaki Kojirō, Musashi would never again kill or even seriously injure an opponent in a skill-match, nor did he ever again use a live blade in them, although he did not mind if his opponents did. Musashi was going ever deeper in his practice and mastery. Somewhat surprisingly, he seems not to have trained Mikinosuke in the martial arts; instead, he put him in the service of Lord Honda.

Leaving Mikinosuke in Himeji, Musashi once again set out travelling, ending up for a time back in Edo. In what was now the de facto capital he may have become acquainted

with a noted Confucian scholar, Hayashi Ranzan, who
served in the administration and was tutor to the first four
Tokugawa shoguns. Whether he was personally acquainted
with him or only by reputation, Hayashi later wrote a
glowing tribute to Musashi. Continuing his travels Musashi
went north, at one point reaching what is now Yamagata
(then part of Dewa province). Sometime during this odyssey
he adopted another son, Iori, but did not teach the martial
arts to him either, at least not to any significant degree, again
preferring to bring him up as a sort of assistant. Musashi was
known to be a brilliant judge of character – he may have
intuited that neither young man was suited to the warrior's
path, and that thriving in a bureaucracy would be the key to
success in the coming years. Or he may simply have wanted
to spare his adopted sons the harsh path he had followed.

Even so, he would not be able to spare Mikinosuke.
Sadly, Lord Honda died aged thirty and Mikinosuke would
follow his lord in *junshi* 殉死, a common practice in which
retainers showed their dedication to their lord by committing
suicide when the liege passed away. This custom was later
forbidden by a Tokugawa edict, but not soon enough to save
Mikinosuke from what he must have seen as a moral duty.
Musashi was in Ōsaka; his son paid him a visit en route back
to Himeji from Edo, and Musashi provided his son with a
lavish feast, no doubt knowing what was to come, although
according to the accounts they never spoke of it directly.

Around the same time Ogasawara Tadazane's fiefdom
had been transferred from Akashi, where Musashi had been

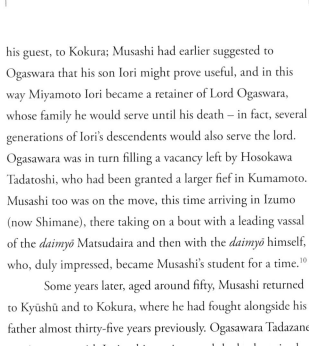

his guest, to Kokura; Musashi had earlier suggested to
Ogaswara that his son Iori might prove useful, and in this
way Miyamoto Iori became a retainer of Lord Ogaswara,
whose family he would serve until his death – in fact, several
generations of Iori's descendents would also serve the lord.
Ogasawara was in turn filling a vacancy left by Hosokawa
Tadatoshi, who had been granted a larger fief in Kumamoto.
Musashi too was on the move, this time arriving in Izumo
(now Shimane), there taking on a bout with a leading vassal
of the *daimyō* Matsudaira and then with the *daimyō* himself,
who, duly impressed, became Musashi's student for a time.[10]

    Some years later, aged around fifty, Musashi returned
to Kyūshū and to Kokura, where he had fought alongside his
father almost thirty-five years previously. Ogasawara Tadazane
was in power, with Iori as his retainer, and the lord received
Musashi with great hospitality. It was while Musashi was here
that, in 1637, food shortages and excessive taxation by a local
daimyō in the Shimabara peninsula to the southwest, in Hizen
(now Nagasaki prefecture), caused a rebellion. Led by the
Christian Amakusa Shiro, a large group of *rōnin* 浪人 ("wave
people" in the sense of "men adrift": masterless samurai),
peasants, women and children occupied the vacant Hara
Castle. Ogasawara's forces were among those called upon by
the shogun to quell the revolt; Musashi, at the lord's request,
accompanied Tadazane's untested son Nagatsugu into the
battle as protector. In this he was successful, as Nagatsugu
returned unharmed and the rebellion was put down, but this
was the last time Musashi would fight on the battlefield.

Around this time, and contrary to the popular image of Musashi as a loner who eschewed the company of women, both the *Bushū Denraiki* and a history of the Yoshiwara pleasure quarters published in 1720 seem to indicate that Musashi had a relationship with at least one courtesan during his occasional visits to Edo. According to the former, Musashi's involvement with an *omoimono*[11] produced a daughter, who tragically died young, leaving him grief-stricken; the latter indicates that a woman by the name of Kumoi was "familiar" with Musashi. Whether Kumoi and the mother of Musashi's child were the same woman is unclear, but these completely independent accounts point to a Musashi not immune to the appeal of the opposite sex.

The influence of Lord Hosokawa Tadatoshi

Not long after Musashi had returned to Kokura, he received an invitation from Hosokawa Tadatoshi to come to Kumamoto, in Higo, where Hosokawa was *daimyō*. Musashi took his time considering the offer, but a year later he took Hosokawa up on it, and moved to Kumamoto, leaving Iori with Ogasawara in Kokura. His hesitation seems to have been one of humility more than anything else; besides being one of the most powerful *daimyō*, Tadatoshi was also an extremely cultured man – a poet and painter as well as a master of *sadō* 茶道 (tea ceremony), having learned that art from none other than Sen no Rikyū himself. In fact, there is some indication that Hosokawa and Musashi had met before at a poetry circle in Kyōto; Musashi, whatever the impression he had made on the *daimyō* then, now pointed out in a letter that he was growing old and recently felt sick – consequently, he would be of little use to Tadatoshi beyond an advisory capacity, although he would be glad to be of assistance if possible. He asked for nothing in the way of status.

What he was given was rather more. He sat at Hosokawa's table as an honoured guest, was quartered comfortably at the old Chiba Castle, and received a substantial stipend even though he was not even officially in the employ of the *daimyō*. Besides being a man of the arts, Tadatoshi also had a keen interest in swordsmanship and was an advanced practitioner. He had been a student of Yagyū Munenori and even received a certificate of transmission in the *Shinkage Ryū*. In fact, a retainer of the Yagyū,[12] Ujii Yashirō, had come to Kumamoto to continue teaching Tadatoshi; the lord arranged a bout between this practitioner of the *Shinkage Ryū* and Musashi. When Musashi quickly bested the Yagyū emissary, Tadatoshi was astounded and jumped in, immediately requesting a bout himself. Himself similarly subdued in a short time, Lord Hosokawa admitted he had never imagined Musashi to be so advanced. From then on he became a student of Musashi's style, which he was now calling the *Ni Ten Ichi Ryū* ("Two Heavens One Style").[13]

Besides Musashi teaching Hosokawa his two-sword style, the two also practised many other arts together, including *sadō*, *shodō* 書道 (brush calligraphy) and *suibokuga* 水墨画 (Indian-ink painting). Lord Hosokawa and Musashi seem to have held each other in high esteem, and while

Musashi claims never to have had a teacher in anything after realizing the Way, it seems certain that Hosokawa exerted a distinct influence. In these days Musashi also paid regular visits to a Buddhist priest named Akiyama Wanao, with whom he wrote poems in the *renga*[14] 連歌 tradition, and otherwise spent a good deal of time on the crafting of such items as saddles, sword-hilts, scabbards, bows, *bokutō* 木刀 (wooden swords), and other pieces of a generally martial nature. Musashi, in fact, had dabbled in the arts from a relatively young age (there is a painting of Bodhidharma[15] signed by him from his stay at a temple as a young man), but it was now that Musashi truly seems to have come into his own as an artist as well as a warrior.

The writing of the *Hyōhō Sanjū-go ka Jō*

Early in year eighteen of the Kanei[16] reign (1641), Musashi wrote down for Lord Hosokawa an overview of his style of strategy, which became known as the *Hyōhō Sanjū-go ka Jō*, or "Thirty-five Articles on Strategy", wherein he outlined a number of points that he would later elaborate on more fully in the *Go Rin no Sho*, but also including some that do not appear in the later work. Sadly, Tadatoshi died two months later. The text was returned to Musashi (or he had another copy), which he apparently then gave to one of his students, Terao Motomenosuke – one of three men Musashi chose to carry on his *Ni Ten Ichi Ryū* style of strategy. Motomenosuke or one of his students seem to have added to the text, as later copies of it include thirty-nine or even forty-two articles

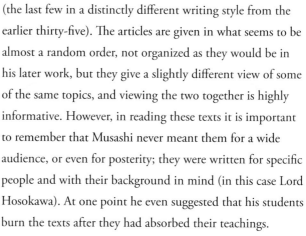

(the last few in a distinctly different writing style from the earlier thirty-five). The articles are given in what seems to be almost a random order, not organized as they would be in his later work, but they give a slightly different view of some of the same topics, and viewing the two together is highly informative. However, in reading these texts it is important to remember that Musashi never meant them for a wide audience, or even for posterity; they were written for specific people and with their background in mind (in this case Lord Hosokawa). At one point he even suggested that his students burn the texts after they had absorbed their teachings.

The death of his friend and patron was a loss no doubt felt keenly by the now ailing Musashi. The following year he began to suffer debilitating pain (it is believed he died of some form of abdominal or thoracic cancer). In 1643 Musashi left his home within the grounds of the old Chiba Castle and moved to Mount Iwato, a few miles to the west of the city. There he divided his time between a local temple (Taishoji), which he lodged near, and a spot connected to it that was known as Reigan-dō 霊厳洞, or "Spirit Rock Cave", and rumoured to have tremendous spiritual powers. He intensified his practice of *zazen* meditation, and began work on the text for which he has become most famous.

The *Go Rin no Sho* ("Writings on the Five Spheres")
Knowing he was not long for this world, Musashi set about writing out the fundamental ideas of his style of strategy for his students. He divided the work into five sections, putting

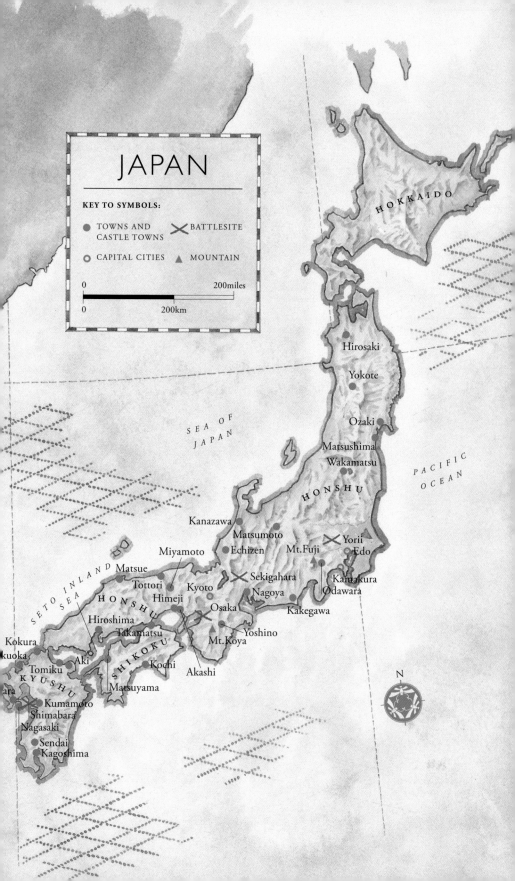

JAPAN

KEY TO SYMBOLS:

● TOWNS AND CASTLE TOWNS ✕ BATTLESITE

◉ CAPITAL CITIES ▲ MOUNTAIN

0   200miles

0   200km

HOKKAIDO

Hirosaki

Yokote

Ozaki

Matsushima
Wakamatsu

SEA OF JAPAN

PACIFIC OCEAN

H O N S H U

Kanazawa

Matsumoto
Echizen

Mt.Fuji

Yorii
Edo

Sekigahara

Kamakura
Odawara

Miyamoto

Matsue

Tottori

Kyoto

Nagoya

Kakegawa

SETO INLAND SEA

H O N S H U

Himeji

Osaka

Hiroshima

Takamatsu

Yoshino

Mt.Koya

Kokura

kuoka

Aki

SHIKOKU

Kochi

Akashi

Tomiku

ara

K Y U S H U

Matsuyama

Kumamoto

Shimabara

Nagasaki

Sendai

Kagoshima

N

each down in a separate scroll: "Earth", in which he explained his own history, the rationale for his writing, a plan for the remaining scrolls, and the basis for all study of his style; "Water", which detailed the specifics of his style of swordsmanship, but included applications to broader strategy; "Fire", which dealt with combat and battle in general; "Wind", wherein he dissected the shortcomings of the other styles of strategy; and finally "Emptiness", a brief and enigmatic discussion of the formlessness that Musashi implied finally was the highest order.

The choice of these titles was by no means haphazard. It reflects a Buddhist catalogue of the elements, or spheres of existence, specifically in the esoteric Shingon tradition.[17] Moreover, memorial reliquaries representing these spheres – Japanese versions of the *stupas* seen elsewhere in Asia, but which in Japan were called *gorintō* 五輪塔 or "five-ring towers" (hence the often-used title "Five Rings") – can be seen all over Japan, and would have been there in Musashi's time as well; by some accounts Musashi also spent some time on Mount Kōya in Wakayama (then the Kii province), the centre of Shingon Buddhism. These pillars have a cubic base representing Earth and solidity, and they ascend – in the same sequence as Musashi's arrangement of his scrolls – in various shapes that represent a progress from solidity to insubstantiality and finally Emptiness. Musashi was said to have wanted "no monument" erected to him, no marker for his grave, but it is clear that in a sense Musashi saw the writing of this text as his "monument".

It is worth noting here that although Musashi claims in "Ground" that he does not "borrow the old Buddhist or Confucian teachings" it may seem that the truth is otherwise. However, it was common in those days for writers to quote, directly and sometimes quite liberally, from the established canon of philosophical texts, and this is almost certainly what Musashi refers to; indeed, he has not quoted from any such texts at all at any length, preferring to put things in his own way. But to say that he has not "borrowed" teachings is not really accurate, for he has included many concepts from the Buddhist, Taoist and Confucian traditions.

Musashi was throughout his life a student of Buddhism,[18] mostly Zen but possibly being influenced by the Shingon tradition, which was practised by the Yagyū, among others.[19] His concept of *kū* 空 or Emptiness comes directly from the Buddhist tradition; it is the sense of the oneness of everything, of formlessness, that comes with emptying one's self of the ego or self-consciousness. Often called *muga-mushin* (無我無心 "no self, no mind"), this is reflected in Musashi's concepts such as the "no thought, no form" strike described in "Water". Even the very subject upon which Musashi writes – *hyōhō* 兵法 ("soldier law" or strategy) – contains within it the Buddhist concept of *hō* 法 or "correct action". Musashi's repeated admonitions for the student to "study this intensively" or "practise this unceasingly", moreover, echo the reflective and rigorous qualities of Zen, right down to the phrasing. He often uses the word *kufū* 工夫, which now means "to make various

adjustments in order to improve", but originally was a Buddhist term meaning "to work through philosophical problems deeply and persistently", to describe how his students should approach the principles he teaches.

The Taoist tradition also figures heavily in Musashi's writing. The idea of the Way (道 – *tao* or *dao* in Chinese; *dō* in the Sino-Japanese *on-yomi* reading, or *michi* in the native Japanese *kun-yomi*) is that of the natural order of the universe, which is manifested through natural principles (*ri* 理, or in Musashi's writing sometimes with the *kanji* 利). The various Ways that Musashi discusses, then, such as the Way of the Carpenter, or the Way of Strategy, are viewed as the practice of those activities or professions as philosophical endeavours, through which the ultimate Way of the universe may be revealed. Another concept of Taoism that is fundamental to Musashi's writing is the division of the universe into the complementary components of *yin* and *yang* (in Japanese called *in* 陰 and *yō* 陽) – the universal female and male, negative and positive, the formless and the solid. This thinking pervades Musashi's conceptual framework, from footwork (the feet move in tandem, like male and female, never just one) to the ways of seeing (perceiving, the objectless *yin* way, and looking, the focused *yang* way), to more abstract psychological aspects like "Moving the Shadows" or "Stifling the Form".

Again, it should be remembered that these concepts would have been very familiar to the audience for which Musashi intended his text. The particular recipient to whom

he addressed the five scrolls of the *Go Rin no Sho* was Terao
Magonojō, brother of Terao Motomenosuke (who eventually
received the "Thirty-five Articles on Strategy") and one of
the three men entrusted with the continuation of the *Ni Ten
Ichi Ryū* school. As accomplished swordsmen who had
trained countless hours with Musashi, these words would
largely have been reminders of what they had already learned
under Musashi's tutelage. Thus to the reader of today, mostly
unfamiliar with the handling of the sword, the example of
an "autumn monkey" might be obscure, but one can easily
imagine Musashi chiding his students for trying to stay far
away from their opponents and hit them from a distance,
gently mocking them as "long-armed monkeys".

In other cases we must remember Musashi's position
as a battle-hardened member of the old guard in a time
when many schools of swordsmanship, being removed from
the battlefield sometimes for generations already, had
become more and more "flowery", in Musashi's words, and
thus ultimately less effective in the event of real combat,
outside of the training hall. Thus his emphasis on treading
firmly on the heels and "floating" (that is, slightly raising)
the tips of the toes: this would assure a stable footing and
avoid snagging the toes on the ground in a situation where
even the slightest stumble could mean the difference
between life and death.

Two years after moving to Mount Iwato and
beginning his meditations at Reigan-dō, Musashi completed
his five scrolls. His hand having become unstable, he had his

friend the priest Akiyama draft a clear copy and check for errors. Musashi had now become too weak to live on his own. He wrote a letter to three top retainers of the Hosokawa, saying he would now seclude himself in the mountains and await death; they apparently felt they could not allow this, and dispatched two men, who had been looking after Musashi, to bring him back to his residence on the grounds of former Chiba Castle in Kumamoto.

In the fifth month of the second year of the Shōhō era (1645) Musashi gathered his closest students and friends, and distributed his various belongings among them. On the twelfth day he dedicated the five scrolls that would later become known as the *Go Rin no Sho* to Terao Magonojō, and to his brother Motomenosuke gave the single scroll of the "Thirty-five Articles on Strategy".[20] In his last days he wrote down a list of twenty-one simple dictates for living an independent life such as his own, a distillation of the hard-earned wisdom he had acquired through his years of living the life of a wandering warrior. He titled it *Dokkōdō* 独行道 – "The Path Walked Alone".

Of these documents, only the *Dokkōdō* exists in the original. According to the *Bushū Denraiki*, the original scrolls of the *Go Rin no Sho* were eventually submitted to the Edo *bakufu* and came to be housed at Edo Castle; they were presumed to be destroyed when the castle burned in 1657, an end that made Musashi's suggestion that his students burn their texts when they had finished with them seem eerily prescient. It is unclear what happened to the original of the "Thirty-five Articles on Strategy", but both it and the five scrolls now sadly seem to exist only as copies.

On the nineteenth, Shinmen Musashi no Kami Fujiwara no Genshin, the great Miyamoto Musashi, died at his home in Kumamoto. His hair was cut and buried near Reigan-dō; as per his instructions, his body was buried in a warrior's armour. Although Musashi is said to have declared that he needed no gravestone, one was in fact erected to him, and ten years after his death his surviving adopted son Iori, who had risen to high status with the Ogasawara, commissioned the priest Akiyama Wanao to write an epitaph for Musashi, which he then had engraved on an imposing monument, known as the Kokura Hibun, that still stands in Kokura.

THE LEGACY OF A MASTERLESS MAESTRO

What was it about Shinmen Musashi that so captured people's imagination? The great Tsukahara Bokuden,[21] founder of the *Kashima Ryū* ("Deer Island Style"), was arguably a greater swordsman, also undefeated but in more than twice as many bouts as Musashi; the Yagyū, Munenori and his kin, were certainly more influential at the time, as instructors to the shoguns. But it was Musashi who truly fascinated the culture at large and cast the longest shadow.

One sure reason was Musashi's status as an iconoclast, in a society that places so much emphasis on conformity and group thinking. All his life, he was essentially a *rōnin*, a "masterless samurai" (although Musashi would likely have preferred the term *bushi* 武士). Although it came in many ways at a great price, Musashi's indomitable sense of freedom was and is no doubt the envy of legions who feel bound by the expectations of their culture, family and society.

The other main aspect is his polymathic quality: many others may have been swordsmen and also practised the gentler arts, but few took to them so quickly or as well. Musashi's works are recognized as masterpieces of calligraphy and Indian-ink painting; his handicrafts are marvels of simple beauty, and all of this is somewhat astounding considering this was a man who devoted the greater portion of his life to mastering the precise application of violence.

An insight into all things
According to Musashi, going deeply into the Way of Strategy produces a revelation of insight into all things, and a freedom in action unlike anything else – once enlightened to the Way, he says in "Ground": "By applying the principles of strategy to the practice of various arts, I have never needed a teacher in any of those things." Thus he was able to turn what he

had learned with swords in hand to the use of the calligraphy brush, the chisel and the implements of the other arts he learned. However, this is not at the level of mere technique: Musashi emphasizes repeatedly the importance of mindset – most importantly, one of Emptiness, of non-attachment, of total freedom – over everything else.

Over the years, Musashi's words have been studied not only by martial artists and military strategists, but also by people across a wide variety of fields, from commerce to the arts. Businessmen have found in it parallels with their own work, viewing competition as a variety of warfare; concepts such as timing, scale and understanding the "battlefield" of the market are all as relevant in today's corporate world as they were to the real battlefield *bushi* of Musashi's day. Musashi, who is fond of such parallels and frequently remarks on the possibility of applying his principles across a variety of situations, would have approved.

Others read him as a model for personal development: a way to live freely and independently. And for everyone and anyone, Musashi's constantly repeated admonitions to "train morning and night", to constantly investigate and work things through – essentially never to stop learning – are reminders of what is truly vital to success in any arena. Musashi indeed seems to have been able to delve so deeply into the Way of combat that he found in it an understanding of the Way of all things, and lived with a fierce and uncompromising intensity. Today, through history, learning about his life and reading the few words this

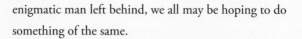

enigmatic man left behind, we all may be hoping to do
something of the same.

About the three Musashi texts

Miyamoto Musashi's *Go Rin no Sho* stands alongside the Zen
priest Takuan Sōhō's *Fudōchishin Myōroku* ("Mysterious
Record of Immovable Wisdom"), the *Hyōhō Kadensho*
("Written Family Transmissions on Strategy") of Yagyū
Munenori, and Yamamoto Tsunetomo's *Hagakure* as one
of the classics of the philosophical tradition in Japanese
swordsmanship. However, in contrast to *Hagakure*, in which
the highest moral calling is service to one's lord unto death,
Musashi's work focuses on the individual, and a way for that
individual to overcome all adversaries. Although Yamamoto
Tsunetomo's work was written later, the ideas in it were
already current when Musashi was writing; in "Ground"
Musashi pointedly indicates his disagreement with the idea
of death in service as the objective of a samurai's life:

> …as far as the Way of Death is concerned, it is not
> limited only to the objectives of warriors: monks,
> women – anyone from peasants on down – can, out
> of duty or shame, take it upon themselves to die. It is
> no different.
>
> In the practice of strategy that is the warrior's
> Way, what is essential is to overcome one's adversary
> no matter what, on whatever the field, whether it be
> in single combat or against multiple opponents, in

order to achieve fame and honour for one's lord and oneself. This [alone] is virtue, in soldiery.

This is resonant with Musashi's own life – never taking a permanent position with any lord, he lived his life relentlessly pursuing his own ends: the perfection of his art. The three texts in this book are guides for strategy, but also essentially for how to live as an individual in the world. Included here are the *Go Rin no Sho* ("Writings on the Five Spheres"), Musashi's magnum opus and summary of his life's learning; the *Hyōhō Sanjū-go ka Jō* ("Thirty-five Articles on Strategy"), written for Lord Hosokawa Tadatoshi two years earlier, which show Musashi's thinking in a developing form; and the *Dokkōdō* ("The Path Walked Alone"), a short list of aphoristic exhortations for how to live life as a warrior, written just before his death.

As has been pointed out, the *Go Rin no Sho* was not written for a general audience but for Musashi's student Terao Magonojō. Although this most famous collection of Musashi's writings is collectively known now by that name, Musashi in fact never gave a title to the work as a whole, but only to the individual scrolls: "Ground", "Water", "Fire", "Wind" and "Emptiness". After Musashi's death it became known variously as "The Writings in Five Scrolls", "The Five Scrolls of Strategy", "The Five Scrolls of Ground–Water–Fire–Wind–Emptiness" and "Writings on the Virtuous Way of Strategy". The direct association with the five-tiered *gorintō*s (and the title "Five Rings") was made by later followers.

As mentioned previously, the original is believed to have been destroyed in a fire at Edo. What material we have today comes from copies that were made by students, recopied and handed down through the various branches of the *Ni Ten Ichi Ryū* school of swordsmanship and strategy. There are two main traditions among the copies, the Higo area school in the Kumamoto area, and the Chikuzen school in Kokura and further north. In preparing this translation I mainly referred to the Hosokawa copy of the text (in the Higo line), but cross-referenced it with other copies in both traditions. Where there are large discrepancies between the copies in the two traditions I have noted this, but have used the Hosokawa version.

The fate of the original version of the *Hyōhō Sanjū-go ka Jō* ("Thirty-five Articles on Strategy") is also unknown. Like the *Go Rin no Sho*, there are various versions, but it is reasonably clear due to differences in content and writing style that the additional articles were added by Musashi's students or even later practitioners after his death, and while these extra pieces are of some historical interest in their own right, I have omitted them in an attempt to limit the contents of this text to material by Musashi himself.

The *Dokkōdō* is the only one of the three texts of which we have a copy in Musashi's own hand. On this faded scroll are Musashi's last written instructions to his students, and to any who would follow his path later; it constitutes the hard-won wisdom from the rigorous and perhaps sometimes lonely life of the "sword-saint".

A NOTE ABOUT TRANSLATION

Musashi's writing style is educated but not the flowery Chinese-styled *kanbun* that was the hallmark of courtly writing at the time (Musashi was of the educated warrior class, but never served as a courtier as such). I have attempted to preserve Musashi's down-to-earth style as I believe it might sound in contemporary English – a mix of the all-business tone of a man who knows his craft and has broad learning in the arts and philosophy besides. I have also attempted to preserve Musashi's syntax and phrasing, insofar as that can be done when translating Japanese into English, and at the same time convey the earthiness of Musashi's expressions that exists in the original. However, there is a great deal of repetition of phrases in the original text; where I felt that English has a number of expressions that convey essentially the same thing, I have varied the phrasing where possible in order to avoid what would doubtlessly become excessive repetitiveness.

Translating these texts into English presents several challenges. For one, both the Japanese of Musashi's time and modern Japanese lack a singular–plural distinction, so it is up to the reader to discern which is the case. Also, in Musashi's Japanese the word *ware* (我) is often used as a subject; this can mean "I", "we" or "the self", and even, by extension, "you" – again, the onus is on the reader to interpret which meaning is intended. Furthermore, the only punctuation used are marks similar to commas, and line breaks. Thus the fitting of Musashi's phrasing into English sentences requires a significant degree of interpretation. However, perhaps the foremost issue is the rendering of a number of frequently used yet ambiguous terms. Some of these, such as *kū* 空 and *dō/michi* 道, have been mentioned, but a few more of these terms are worth some additional explanation. For *dō/michi* at different points I have used alternative words: "way" (not capitalized) is differentiated as simply a method or technique of doing something, whereas "Way" (capitalized) is used to represent cases where a philosophical system is being indicated. In other cases I have used "path", when the term is used to designate an actual physical route.

Musashi's topic itself is 兵法, read either *heihō* or *hyōhō*, the characters of which are literally "soldier" and "law" (the use noted previously of this second character). This term had come to mean "strategy" in general, even before it was imported from China, and although it could be more narrowly interpreted as "soldiery", given Musashi's emphasis on the broad view that seemed too limited in most cases. However, as Musashi himself notes, at the time the word was also widely used to indicate "swordsmanship", and in the cases where it is clear Musashi is using it as such I have translated it with this word. Similarly, the words *hyōhōsha/heihōsha* (兵法者) are rendered as "strategist" or simply "swordsman" or "fighter", depending on whose appraisal is implied – that of a real practitioner of strategy or of an uninformed layman who sees both "strategy" and "swordsmanship" as the same thing.

Read *shin* in its Sinitic reading and *kokoro* in the native Japanese *kun-yomi*, 心 is an extremely broad concept encompassing "heart", "mindset", "mind", "center", "intention", and even "meaning". I have generally rendered this as "mindset", as that is the sense in which it is used most frequently by Musashi, but depending on the context I have translated it with these other words. In some places where I felt the meaning is not well conveyed in English I have noted the use of this word. A final term that causes some difficulty in English translation is *ri*. This word, for which Musashi generally uses the character 利, often means "advantage" or "profit", but sometimes is used interchangeably with another character, 理, also read *ri*, meaning [natural] "principle". Many other terms are problematic to translate into idiomatic English, but do not occur so frequently; I have dealt with other particularly ambiguous or unfamiliar lexicon in many of the endnotes.

I am deeply grateful to my teacher in the *Ni Ten Ichi Ryū*, Washio Kenshin, for his many years of instruction and for his explanation of particularly difficult passages in Musashi's texts in preparing these translations. Without his patience and guidance none of this would have been possible. Any errors or inconsistencies in the translation, however, are mine alone.

PART I

GO RIN NO SHO

"Writings on the Five Spheres"

GROUND

地

My way of military strategy I call the *Ni Ten Ichi Ryū*
[Two Heavens One Style [1]].

Having trained for many years, for the first time
I have thought to explain it in writing. Now, near the
beginning of the tenth month of the twentieth year of
Kanei,[2] I have climbed Mount Iwato, in Higo,[3] Kyūshū.
Here I have exalted Heaven, bowed down before [the
bodhisattva] Kannon,[4] and now face the Buddha. Born in
Harima,[5] I am Shinmen Musashi no kami Fujiwara no
Genshin, a warrior. I am sixty years of age.

Starting in my youth long ago, I set my heart on
following the path of warfare. At thirteen, I fought my first
bout; my opponent was a warrior of the *Shintō* Style called
Arima Kihei, and I defeated him. Then at age sixteen I struck
down a powerful fighter known as Akiyama, of Tajima. At
twenty-one I went up to the capital, where I encountered
many famous swordsmen, and even though I engaged in
numerous duels, never once was I unable to achieve victory.
Following that I went to various regions and places, and met
with the practitioners of different styles. Although I fought
in sixty-odd matches, never did I lose. All of this happened
between the ages of thirteen and twenty-eight or -nine.

When, sometime after I turned thirty, I thought back
over my past, I realized that I had not won all those bouts
because I had achieved great levels of strategic skill. It could
have been because I had some innate gift for this path, and
thus did not get away from its natural principles, or because
those other styles of swordsmanship were lacking in some

respect. After seeing this, in order to attain the deeper principles I set myself to training day in and day out. In due course I realized the Way of Strategy. This was when I was about fifty years old.

Since then I have never again needed to search for the Way in anything. By applying the principles of strategy to the practice of various arts, I have never needed a teacher in any of those things. Thus in writing this book I do not borrow the old Buddhist or Confucian teachings, nor have I any need of the chronicles of military history or treatises on tactics. In order to convey the true heart of this One Style,[6] and taking the Way of Heaven and the *bodhisattva* Kannon as mirrors, on this the night of the tenth day of the tenth month, at the hour of the tiger, I take up my brush and begin to write.[7]

This thing called "strategy" is the practice of the warrior class. Those who command must carry out this practice, and those who fight should also understand this path. In today's world, though, nowhere are there any warriors who can be said to fully understand the Way of Strategy. If you think about it, there are a variety of Ways. Buddhism is the Way of Saving People; the Confucian Way is that which correctly guides those on the Way of Study. The person called a doctor practises the Way of Curing Illness, and then there is the poet, who teaches the Way of Verse. There are also the connoisseur, the archer and the practitioners of many other arts and skills, who all practise as they see fit, and as is their liking.

Few, however, care to follow the path of the warrior. First of all, a warrior has what are called the Dual Paths of Scholarship and Warfare [*Bun Bu Ni Dō*] to follow, and must have a liking for both of these Ways. Even if he is physically clumsy and unsuited for this path, a man of the warrior class must put that aside and train diligently in the ways of soldiery.

Furthermore, if you ask a warrior of one of the great houses what he truly thinks, he will tell you that the warrior must simply acquire a taste for what might be called the Way of Death. However, as far as the Way of Death is concerned, it is not limited only to the objectives of warriors: monks, women – anyone from peasants on down[8] – can, out of duty or shame, take it upon themselves to die. It is no different.

In the practice of strategy that is the warrior's Way, what is essential is to overcome one's adversary no matter what, on whatever the field, whether it be in single combat or against multiple opponents, in order to achieve fame and honour for one's lord and oneself. This [alone] is virtue, in soldiery.

There are, though, probably some people in the world who think that even if they learn the Way of Strategy, when the real time comes, it will be of no use.

With regard to this opinion: To train so that it will be useful at any time, and to teach so that it will be useful in all things – this is the true Way of Strategy.

Regarding the Way of Strategy

From China to Japan, those who pursue this Way are known as "experts in strategy"; not to study these methods is unthinkable for members of the warrior class.

地

These days, everywhere there are people who go around calling themselves "practitioners of strategy", but they only know swordsmanship. In the province of Hitachi, priests at both the Kashima and Kantori shrines,[9] claiming to have received instruction directly from the gods, have established styles, and travel from region to region teaching them to people. This is a recent thing. From long ago we have had the Ten Abilities and Seven Arts,[10] and "Achieving Advantage" is known as one of the Arts, but this certainly is not limited to swordsmanship alone. With what is gained from just fencing, it is hard even to understand swordsmanship itself, and of course you will not realize the true principles of strategy.

地

Looking around the world, you see the various arts being sold as commodities, and people even thinking of themselves as goods for sale, and when they make their equipment,

they think of that as something to sell as well. This is like separating the flower from the fruit, with the fruit here being quite less than the flower. Especially in the martial arts, colourful and flowery displays of technique are made, and people talk of this *dōjō* or that *dōjō*, teach this Way or learn that one, hoping to gain profit of some kind from it.

Someone said that "immature strategy is the source of great injuries", and this is absolutely true.

Ordinary people[11] usually take one of four paths through life: that of the farmer, merchant, warrior or artisan.[12]

地

First is the Way of Farming. The farmer gathers his tools and, carefully watching the changes in the four seasons, sees the years in and out. This is the Way of Farming.

地

Second is the Way of Business. For example, the *sake* brewer assembles the various materials he needs, profits according to their quality, and thus makes his way through life. No matter what the path of commerce, all merchants make their living from the profits they make in selling things, and in this way go through the world. This is the Way of Business.

地

Third, regarding the warrior of the samurai class, he must prepare an assortment of weapons and understand the specific virtues of each. This is the Way of the Warrior. Without handling the weapons and becoming accustomed to them, it is impossible to realize their individual advantages, and this would make the refinements of the warrior clans somewhat shallow, wouldn't it? [13]

地

Fourth is the Way of Technical Skill. Consider the way of the

carpenter: he must become adept with all kinds of tools, and understand their specific utility. Taking his square and plumb line he quickly and correctly builds from the plans; using these techniques he makes his way in the world.

Military strategy can be explained by comparing it to the way of the carpenter, and discussing the thing called a "house". We talk about noble houses, the houses of the warrior clans, the Four Houses[14] – the destruction[15] of those houses, or their continuation. We also speak of this school or that tradition in terms of "houses", and when talking about houses it makes sense to compare these things to the way of the carpenter. Also, the word carpenter is written with the characters "great" and "skill";[16] since the Way of Strategy too requires great skill, I have chosen to liken it to that of the carpenter. If you want to learn the practice of war, use these writings as a guide for your thinking. With the master as needle and the disciple as thread, you must train unceasingly.

地

Comparing the Way of Strategy to that of the carpenter

A general, like a head carpenter, must understand the

measure of all things: he must investigate the lay of the country and know the measure of his house's influence. This is the Way of Leadership.

The head carpenter must know how to lay out temples, pagodas, and monasteries with his plumb line, and understand the plans for palaces, manors, towers and fortresses. In that when putting up houses he makes use of various people, the head of a team of carpenters is the same as the head of a samurai clan.

In building a house, the lumber must be allocated. Straight wood without knots, and which looks good, is used in the exterior pillars. Timber that is slightly knotted but straight and strong can be used for interior pillars. Wood that is a little weak but which has no knots and looks nice has various uses in sills, lintel-pieces, doors and *shōji*.[17] Even if it is knotty and gnarled, if the wood is strong it can be used, and as long as the strengths of the house are analyzed and carefully assessed, that house will be long-lasting and unlikely to collapse. If among the lumber there is wood that is knotty, warped and weak, it can be used in scaffolds, and afterwards should become firewood.

The leader, in employing his carpenters, must know their relative abilities, and assign this one to make alcoves, that one to make sliding paper doors, certain ones to make doorsills, lintel-pieces, ceilings and so forth. The unskilled he has lay out the joists, and those even worse he has make wedges. If he distinguishes between his people when he uses them, things will go quickly and efficiently.

Determination in action. Efficiency. Vigilant attention to details. Comprehending form and function.[18] Understanding high, middle and low levels of energy, and how to create morale. Apprehending the intangibles. Everything of this kind – these are all things that are in the mindset of the head carpenter. The principles of military strategy are the same.

地

The Way of soldiery

Like a footsoldier, the carpenter sharpens his tools by hand, assembles them and puts them in his carpenter's box to carry them. He goes where the head carpenter tells him to, and with his adze he hews pillars and beams; with his plane he shaves down the floors and shelves. He does both openwork and carvings, measuring carefully, applying his well-developed skills down to the finest details – this is the

GROUND

55

practice of carpentry. By applying his hands to the techniques of the carpenter and learning them, and understanding building plans well, later he can become a head carpenter himself.

地

As a carpenter, it is crucial to have tools that can cut well, and to sharpen them whenever there is a little time. Taking up these tools and making portable shrines or bookshelves, tables, or lanterns, or cutting boards, or lids for pots – making all of these skillfully is the special work of the carpenter. Being a soldier is similar; you should consider this seriously. For the carpenter, that the wood not be allowed to twist, that the corners fit squarely, that he planes well, but not so far that the wood warps later on – all of this is essential. If you are thinking about learning the Way of Strategy, you should read what is written here, paying attention to every detail, and examine it well.

地

Preparing these writings on strategy in five scrolls

I have divided these principles into five Ways, with one section for each, and in order to explain their various aspects, am writing them out as the five scrolls of "Ground", "Water", "Fire", "Wind" and "Emptiness".

With regard to the "Ground" scroll, it presents the general ideas of the Way of Strategy, and the perspective of my individual style. Through swordsmanship alone, it is difficult to attain the true Way – from large things you must understand the small, and from the shallow you can arrive at the deep. In that it is like a straight path drawn across the terrain, the first I have named the "Ground" scroll.

Second is the "Water" scroll, taking water as its basis, as the mind becomes like water: water takes on the shape of whatever container it fills, be it angled or round, and can be a single drop or a vast ocean. There is a colour of deepest blue in water, and with its purity as a model I write out an explanation of my individual style in this scroll.

If you discern the underlying principles of swordsmanship clearly, when you are able to freely defeat a single opponent, you can beat anyone in the world. The mindset[19] that overcomes one enemy, or a thousand, or ten thousand,[20]

is the same. The strategy of the commander translates the small into the large, just like taking a model of one *shaku*[21] and from it building a giant statue of the Buddha.

地

Things like this are difficult to write about in detail. Having one thing, to understand ten thousand – this is an underlying principle of Strategy. I write about my own particular style in this "Water" scroll.

地

Third is the scroll of "Fire", and in this scroll I write specifically about combat. Since, like fire, combat can be both large and small, and has such a ferocious spirit, I write about engaging in battle here.

地

The Way of Battle: whether man-to-man combat, or a battle of ten thousand against ten thousand, the Way is the same. Your mind sometimes becoming expansive and sometimes small-scale, you must look at this, examining it carefully.

The large is easily seen; the small is hard to see. This is because large numbers of men cannot easily be redirected at once, whereas an individual, having only one mind, can thus change very rapidly. For this reason, it is difficult to acquire

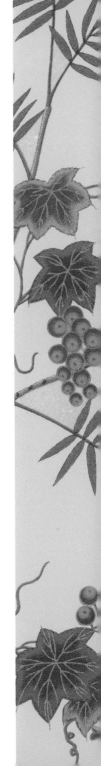

an understanding of the small scale. You need to investigate this thoroughly. This "Fire" scroll explains how – because of the instantaneous nature of battle – to train daily, to think of combat as being just like your everyday life, and to have an unwavering spirit, all are vital in strategy. Accordingly I write about battle and single combat in the "Fire" scroll.

Fourth is the "Wind" scroll. In this scroll I entitle "Wind",[22] I do not discuss my own particular style, but instead here write about the various other schools of strategy in the world today. When we speak of a "wind" [meaning "style"], we talk about

"old style", "modern style", or the style of this house or that one; I write explicitly about the techniques of the assorted schools of strategy that are around, so this part is called "Wind".

If you do not understand others, it is difficult to analyze yourself. In all Ways and in every instance, there are thoughts that "deviate from the Way", as they are called. Even if you can say that you are striving hard every day on a particular Way, if your heart strays from it, though you may think it is a good path, when viewed objectively it is not the true Way.

If you do not perfect the true Way, and your mindset becomes slightly skewed, later it may become greatly awry – you should examine this.

Other schools of "strategy" most people think of as being just swordsmanship, and this is understandable; however, the principles and techniques of my own strategy have a different meaning. In order to explain what is known in the world as "strategy", I call this scroll "Wind", and in it write about the other styles.

Fifth is the scroll of "Emptiness". In writing about

"emptiness" in this scroll, since I am talking about
"emptiness", there is nothing to be called the "depths" or
to be called the "entrance".[23] Once you have acquired the
principles of the Way, you let go of them. In the Way
of Strategy you become naturally free, and gain an
extraordinary power: you understand the appropriate
rhythm for any given moment, spontaneously strike, and
naturally hit your mark. All this is the Way of Emptiness.
How one naturally enters the true Way I put in writing
as the scroll of "Emptiness".

Naming this particular style "Two Swords"

We talk about "the two swords": the position of members
of the warrior class, from generals to footsoldiers, is one in
which two swords are worn at the belt from the outset.
In the old days they were called *tachi* and *katana*; now they
are called the *katana* and *wakizashi*.[24]
There is no need to write the particulars about the wearing
of these two swords. Here in our country, no matter whether
one understands it or not, wearing them is the way of
a member of the warrior class. In order to indicate
the fundamental principle of these two, I call this the
Ni Tō Ichi Ryū [Two Swords One Style[25]].

地

The spear, the pole-sword [*naginata*[26]] and so forth
we will leave aside, although they are also among the
tools of war – the way of this style is for even the beginner
to take both the long and the short sword,[27] one in each
hand, and practise the Way. This is the true point: when
you lay down your life, you want to make use of all your
implements, without leaving any unused. Not to make use
of a weapon, and to die with it still in its scabbard at your
hip, is a truly unthinkable thing.

地

Not only that, but if you hold something with both your
hands, it is difficult to use it freely to both the right and left,
so you have to get used to using the long sword in one hand.
With big weapons such as the spear or *naginata* it cannot be
helped, but as for the *katana* and *wakizashi*, they are both
weapons meant to be held in one hand. It is generally bad to
hold the long sword with both hands – bad on horseback,
and bad when running, bad in swamps, in wet rice paddies,
on rocky terrain, or in crowds of people.
When you are holding a bow or spear in your left hand, or
holding any other tool for that matter, you always have to
use the sword one-handed, so taking position with the long
sword in both hands is not in the true Way. However, in
times when it is difficult to strike and kill a man with one

hand, you should [go ahead and] cut him down with two;
it shouldn't be something that causes you a lot of worry.

Because at first one is not accustomed to wielding the sword
in one hand, we take up two swords, and in this way learn
how to swing the long sword one-handed. Although for
everyone, when they start, the *tachi* is heavy and hard to
swing around, all things are so at the beginning: the bow is
hard to draw, and the *naginata* is difficult to wield. Any of
the weapons takes getting used to. You become able to draw
the bow with strength, and when you are accustomed to
swinging the long sword, you understand the power of its
Way, and it becomes easy to wield.

As for the Way of the long sword, swinging it fast is not a

part. In the "Water" scroll I explain this. The long sword is for use in large spaces, the short sword for use in confined spaces – first and foremost, this is the fundamental idea of this Way. In this style, you win with long, and you win with short. Therefore there is no need to establish a particular length for our long sword.[28] The mindset of "achieve victory, no matter what" – that is the way of *this* style.

There are times when it is better to wield two swords than one: when fighting singly against a crowd, or when taking a hostage, it is advantageous. There is no need to write about things like this specifically at this point. Having one thing, you should know ten thousand. Practise and achieve the Way of Strategy, and there will never be a single thing you do not see. You should investigate this extensively.

Understanding the principles of the two characters in the word "strategy"[29]

Talking about this Way, most people call those who have acquired the ability to wield a sword "strategists". In the

Ways of the Martial Arts,[30] if you can shoot a bow well, you are called an "archer"; one who has learned to shoot a gun is known as a "gunner"; one who uses a spear, a "spearman"; and one who has learned the pole-sword, a "pole-swordsman". And yet, someone who has learned the Way of the Sword is not called a "longswordsman" or "shortswordsman". The bow, the gun, the spear and the *naginata*: all these are tools of the warrior, and each of them part of the Way of Strategy; however, there is a reason why the long sword specifically is referred to when we speak of strategy. Since it is by virtue of the sword that the world is controlled, and that one controls oneself, the sword is the place from which strategy begins.

地

If the virtue of the long sword is grasped, one man can defeat ten. If one man can defeat ten, then a hundred can defeat a thousand, or a thousand defeat ten thousand. In my style of strategy, one man or ten thousand are the same thing; it can be said of this strategy that nothing in the warrior's practice is left out.

地

As far as Ways go, those of the Confucian, the Buddhist, the tea master, the master of etiquette, the Noh dancer – these are not in the warrior's Way. But even though I say they are

not part of this Way, if you understand the Way broadly, you will find it in all things. For each person, to carefully polish his own Way – that's what is essential.

Knowing the advantages of weapons in strategy

If you are able to discern the advantages of the implements of war, then you can use each of these tools fittingly, according to the time and place. The short sword is of advantage when in a narrow space, or when right up next to an opponent. The long sword, used in any situation, generally has advantages. The *naginata*, on the battlefield, seems inferior compared to the spear. The spear is for attacking; the *naginata* brings up the rear. With the same level of training, the spear is a little stronger, but it depends on the situation – in confined spaces, neither is of much use, nor is either much good for taking prisoners. They are only really implements for the battlefield, but when engaging in battle they are vital tools.

However, if you learn the principles of these weapons indoors,[31] and focus on learning trivial specifics, forgetting

about the true Way, then it will be very hard to apply
any of them appropriately.

As for the place of the bow in battle, it is appropriate
for when troops advance or retreat. When paired with spears
or used in tandem with other weapons, since it can be shot
rapidly, it is an especially good thing to use in situations
such as battles on open fields. It is an insufficient tool
for besieging a castle, or at distances from the enemy
exceeding twenty *ken*.[32]

In the present world it goes without saying for the bow,
and all the other arts, that there are a lot of flowers but not
much fruit. This kind of skill, in the crucial moment,
will not be of much use.

From inside a castle or other fortification, there is nothing
to rival a gun. Also, in situations such as the open field,
before the battle is met, it has numerous advantages.
Once the battle starts it becomes less effective. Surely, one
of the virtues of the bow is that an arrow when shot can be
seen by the human eye. That the bullet from a gun cannot

be seen by the eye is a drawback. You should study
the significance of this.

Regarding horses, it is vital that they should be strong and
durable, and without quirks. Like all the implements of
war, the horse too should be driven broadly; the long and
short swords should cut broadly, the spear and *naginata*
thrust in large movements, the bow and gun shoot
powerfully and not break easily.

You should not discriminate against or develop special
likings for certain weapons, or anything else. Too much
of any one thing is the same as not enough.

Without imitating other people, choose what is appropriate
for your own size and shape; you should have weapons that
you can wield comfortably. For generals or footsoldiers,
to like or dislike certain things is bad. Being adaptable
and inventive is vital.

Regarding rhythm in strategy

While in all things there is rhythm, the rhythm of strategy requires extensive training to master. The rhythms of the world are expressed in such things as the Way of Dance and the rhythms of wind and string musicians; in all these, there is a harmonized and peaceful rhythm. Moving over to the Ways of the Martial Arts: the shot of a bow, the firing of a gun, and the riding of a horse all have rhythms and timings. In all skills and abilities, rhythm is a thing that should not be ignored. Furthermore, there is also rhythm in that which is empty.

地

In the career of a warrior, there is a rhythm to rising in service to one's master, and a rhythm to falling from favour, a rhythm to things going as expected, and a rhythm to the unexpected happening. Or, in the Way of Business, there is a rhythm to becoming wealthy, and a rhythm to wealth disappearing; in every Way there are different rhythms. In all things, the rhythms in which they thrive, and the rhythms in which they decline – you should carefully discern these.

地

There are a variety of rhythms in strategy. First of all, understanding the matching rhythm and distinguishing it from the rhythm which does not match, and from among

rhythms large and small, slow and fast, understanding the
rhythm of hitting the mark, understanding the rhythm of
intervals, and understanding the rhythm that goes against
rhythm – these are the most essential things in strategy.
If you do not get how to discern the rhythm of opposition,
your strategy will never be certain.

In a battle of strategy, understand your opponents' rhythms,
and have rhythms that your adversaries are unable to predict
– the rhythms of emptiness, which proceed from the rhythm
of wisdom – and victory will follow.

In each of these scrolls I write about the subject of
rhythm expressly; investigating what I have written here,
you must train rigorously.

Practising every morning to night in the Way of Strategy
– the particular style discussed above [33] – my mindset
naturally became broad. A strategy for both the large and the
small scale, I now transmit it to the world, putting it down
in writing for the first time in these five scrolls: "Ground",
"Water", "Fire", "Wind" and "Emptiness".

地

To those people who want to learn my strategy, there are
these rules for practising the Way:

Make your thinking free of evil.
Train diligently in the Way.
Become familiar with all of the arts.
Understand the Ways of all the professions.
In all things, discern profit from loss.
Learn to evaluate everything.
Realize and understand that which cannot be seen.
Notice even the slightest thing.
Don't do things that serve no purpose.

Taking these broad principles to heart, you should train
diligently in the Way of Strategy. In this Way specifically,
if you do not take a broad view and see the correct elements,
it is virtually impossible to become a master of strategy.
However, if you study and understand these laws, this is
a Way in which even alone you should not lose to twenty
or thirty adversaries.

First of all, if you fix your attention unceasingly on strategy and work hard on the true Way, you will not only conquer with your technique, but defeat people just by looking in their eyes. Moreover, when with this training you have total control and freedom of your body, you can use your body to defeat people, or, having the spirit that comes from being trained in this Way, defeat others just with that spirit. Upon reaching this point, how can you be defeated by anyone?

Furthermore, as strategy on a large scale, one wins by retaining good people, and by using large numbers of them; one is victorious by way of comporting oneself correctly, by governing the country, by nurturing the people, and by carrying out the laws of the world. On any given path, knowing how not to lose out to others, how to help oneself, and to establish one's reputation – this is the Way of Strategy.

Shōhō [Era] Second Year,[34] Fifth Month, Twelfth Day
Shinmen Musashi
[to] Terao Magonojō [honorific][35]

Kanbun [Era] Seventh Year,[36] Second Month, Fifth Day
Terao Yumeyo Katsunobu
[given to] Yamamoto Gennosuke [honorific][37]

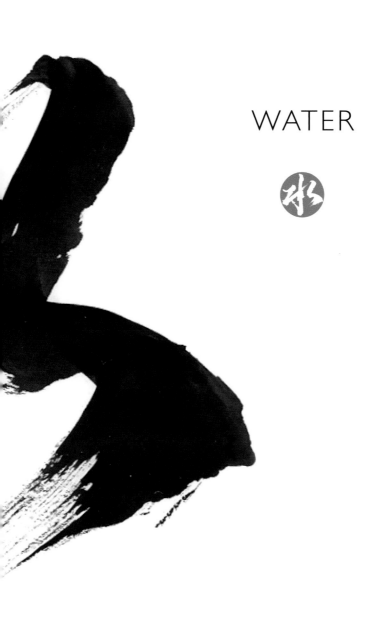

WATER

The strategy of the *Ni Ten Ichi Ryū* [Two Heavens One Style] is at its heart based on water. Putting into practice a method of achieving advantage, in these writings [that I call] the scroll of "Water", I record the handling of the sword in this style.

In any case, it is difficult to explain the heart of this Way in detail without somehow changing it. However, even though – as I say – words are not sufficient, you will understand the deep principles for yourself, as a matter of course.

What is written here – each thing – you should reflect on, word by word. If you think about it carelessly, there are many things in the Way that are misunderstood.

The principles of strategy I have written out here relate to one-on-one combat, but in order also to grasp the principles of a battle of ten thousand against ten thousand, it is crucial to take a broad view.

On this Way [of Strategy], if you view the path incorrectly or stray from it – even a little – you will fall into bad ways. Just looking at these writings is not sufficient to realize the Way of Strategy. Take into your very self the things written here, not thinking of them as something to read or learn, or to imitate, but as principles you have discovered within your own heart, and thoroughly investigate and experiment with them daily.

Mindset in strategy

In the Way of Strategy, your mindset should not differ from your everyday mind. In daily life or in strategic moments, without changing it even the slightest bit, make your mind broad and straight. Without trying to rein it in tightly, or letting it go slack at all, and in such a way that it does not lean in any particular direction, centre your mind exactly, and set it quietly vibrating. You should investigate this exhaustively, until you can sustain this vibration constantly, and not allow it to cease even for a split second.[1]

At quiet times, your mind should not become quiet, and when for some reason you are hurried, your mind should not become even a little rushed. Your mindset should not be affected by your body, nor your body by your mind.

Pay close attention to the state of your mind, and do not worry about your body – fill any places where your mind is lacking, but do not allow it to become overfull at all.

While relaxing the surface of your mind, make its depths strong, not allowing others to discern your mindset.

Understand thoroughly how a small body can be large
in spirit, and know completely how a large body can be
small in spirit; whether large or small, set your mind
straight – having a mind that is not controlled by your
body is essential.[2]

Do not allow your mind to become clouded, but make it
expansive, and in this broadness you should place your
wisdom. It is of utmost importance to polish both your
wisdom and your mindset devotedly.

Honing your wisdom, you will recognize what is right and
wrong in any situation, and understand the good and bad of
everything; knowing every art and skill, and being familiar
with every Way, when you have achieved a condition where
you cannot be tricked by anyone in the world in the tiniest
way – that is the wisdom at the heart of strategy.

In the wisdom of the Way of Strategy, there is something
unlike anything else. You must investigate this thoroughly,

refining the principles of the Way of Strategy until in battle, even when everything is in chaos, your mind is unshakeable.

Comportment in strategy

As for holding the body, the face should be tilted neither down nor up; it should not be scowling and the eyes should not bulge out. Do not wrinkle your forehead, but set a crease between the brows so that you do not blink or move your eyeballs; narrow your eyes a little, and soften your gaze placidly. The line of the nose should be straight, with a slight feeling of sticking out the chin. Straighten the sinews at the back of the neck, putting a feeling of energy into the hairline there.

Thinking of the body from the shoulders down as being all of a piece, lower your shoulders and make your back straight, without letting your buttocks stick out. Extend your energy down from your knees to the tips of your feet. So that you do not stoop over at the waist, expand your abdomen, thrusting it forwards somewhat. There is the teaching called "tightening the wedge" – set your belly against the scabbard of your short sword so that your belt does not slacken; this is "tightening the wedge".

All in all, regarding your physical carriage in strategy, it is vital to make your normal, everyday posture your strategic posture, and make your strategic stance your usual stance. You must investigate this thoroughly.

Setting the gaze in strategy

In setting the gaze, make it large and set it broadly. There are two kinds of gaze: perceiving and looking. The gaze that perceives is strong; the gaze that looks is weak. To see faraway things as if they were close, and to see things that are close as though they were far away, is key in strategy.

To understand your opponent's sword, but not to look at it at all – it can be said that this, too, is an extremely important thing in strategy. This takes serious practice.

This setting of the gaze, in small-scale strategy and in large, is the same. Without moving your eyes,[3] see both of your flanks. This is crucial. Things of this sort are very hard to

figure out all at once, under pressure.[4] Learn what is written here, and make this your main, everyday way of seeing. You should carefully refine this until your gaze does not change in any situation.

Grasping the sword

When taking up the sword, hold it with a floating feeling in your thumb and first finger, the middle finger neither tight nor loose, and grasp it with the feeling of tightening the ring and little fingers. A loose feeling in the grip is bad.

You should take up the sword thinking of it as a thing for cutting down your opponent. When you cut down your adversary, your grasp does not change; hold it in such a way that your hand does not become frozen.

Although there are times when you also block, parry, hit, or press down your adversary's sword, only alter your thumb and index finger, and even then with the feeling of only changing slightly; in any case, you must hold the sword with the intention of cutting. The grip used when test-cutting[5] and the grip used when cutting in combat is the same "person-cutting grip"; it does not change.

Overall, whether with respect to the sword or your hand, you should dislike a feeling of it being settled in one place or position. A settled hand is a dead hand. One that does not become settled is a living hand. This is a thing you need to take to heart thoroughly.

Using the feet [6]

As for moving the feet – "floating" the tips of the toes slightly, you should tread firmly on your heels. Although depending on circumstances there are large, small, slow, or fast strides, the feet should be used just as when walking normally. "Flying" feet, "floating" feet, "creeping" feet: these three types of footwork are to be avoided.

Regarding our Way, it is very important to say this: what is called "*yin–yang* footwork" is absolutely essential. In *yin–yang* footwork, there is no moving of just one foot. When cutting, when retreating, or when advancing, just as *yin* and *yang* alternate, the feet tread right–left–right–left. There shouldn't be any repeatedly stepping with the same foot. This is something that needs to be examined closely.

The five positions

The five orientations of position are: raised, middle, lowered, to the right side and to the left side – these are the five orientations.[7] Even divided into five types, the positions are all for the purpose of cutting a person down. Beyond these five positions, there are no others.

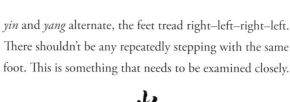

In taking any position, do not think of "taking up a
position" – you should think only of cutting.

Taking a larger or smaller stance will depend on the
situation and should follow from principle.

The raised, middle and lowered positions
are "solid" positions; those to the sides are
"fluid" positions. The right and left positions
are for circumstances such as where one is
blocked in above, or blocked at one side.
The right and left are decided according to location.

In this Way, it is especially important for you to understand
that the middle is the ultimate position. The middle is the
original meaning of "position". Look at large-scale strategy:
the middle position is the general's seat. The other four
positions follow the general's orders.

Investigate this diligently.

水

The path of the sword

To speak of understanding the path of the long sword
that we usually wear: even when swung with two fingers,
if you understand the path[8] of the sword well,
it can be wielded freely.

水

If you try to swing the long sword quickly, it goes against
the natural movement of the sword and is difficult to
swing. In order to wield it well, the sword should be
swung with a feeling of moving it calmly. If you try to
use it like a fan,[9] or like a dagger,[10] intending to move
it quickly, this goes against the natural movement of the
sword and makes it hard to wield. This is called
"dagger chopping", and you cannot cut a person
down with a sword in this way.

水

When you strike downwards with the sword, raise it up in
a path it takes easily, and when you swing it horizontally,
return it horizontally in its natural path – always broadly
extending your elbows, and swinging powerfully; this is the
natural path of the sword.

WATER

93

If you use, and by using learn, the five standard forms you
will establish the natural path of the sword and be able
to wield it easily. You should train diligently.

The progression of five standard forms[11]

The First Form

The position for the first form is the middle height, directing
the tips of your swords to the opponent's face. As you and
your adversary approach each other, when the opponent cuts
at your long sword, slip it to the right and "ride" the
adversary's sword with your long sword. When the opponent
tries to cut again, turn the tips of your swords[12] and cut down
at him, leaving your swords lowered just as they are [at the
end of the downwards cut]. Then when again the adversary
cuts, strike his hands from below. This is the first form.

As a rule, you cannot comprehend these five forms just on
the basis of what is written [here]. To understand the five
forms, take the swords in your hands and practise their

natural path. With the path of the swords found in these five forms, no matter what sword [technique] your opponent strikes with, you will understand it. As for the positions of the two swords, apart from these five there are no others, it should be noted here. You must forge your skills through discipline.

The Second Form

The swords in the second form are in the raised position. From there, cut down at the adversary once, just as he is about to strike.

If you miss your opponent, leave your swords [lowered] just as they are, and when the enemy strikes again, strike him by scooping up from below. If he strikes again, do the same thing.

Within these techniques there can be a wide variety of "feeling" and rhythm, but if, applying what is [found] within these techniques, you train in this style and come to understand the five paths of the sword very precisely, you will have victory in any situation. You must practise.

The Third Form

For the position in the third form, hold the swords in the lowered position with the feeling of letting them hang there. At the moment your adversary goes to strike, hit at his hands from below. When the opponent attempts to strike down your swords as they hit at his hands, come up over his sword in a forestalling rhythm[13] after he has swung, with the intent of cutting laterally across his upper arms.

With the lowered position, it is all about striking and stopping the enemy's strike all at once, just as he strikes. The lowered position is often employed when following the Way [of Swordsmanship[14]], both in times when you move fast and when you move slowly. Taking up the swords, you must train with discipline.

The Fourth Form

For the position of the fourth form, take a position with the swords to the left side. You should hit the opponent's hands from below as he goes to strike. If the adversary tries to knock

down your rising attack, with the feeling of striking his hands
parry the path of his sword in the same way, and cut upwards
at an angle with the long sword to above your own shoulder
height. This is the natural path of the sword.

When the attacker comes to strike, understanding[15] the
path of the [opponent's] long sword is the way to victory.
You should test this thoroughly.

The Fifth Form

For the fifth form, take a position with the swords sideways
to your right side. When you realize that your opponent
is taking up a stance to attack, swing the long sword up at
an angle from the lower side to a raised position,
then directly cut from above.

This [form] is also to familiarize the student with the natural
path of the swords. If using this technique you become

accustomed to swinging the swords; you will then be
able to wield even a heavy sword freely.

It is impossible to write out these five forms in detail.
The aim of this style is basically to understand the natural
path of the sword, and also to learn the general rhythms [of
combat], and become able to perceive the opponent's sword.

First of all, using these five techniques, train your hands
unceasingly. Also, when in combat with an opponent,
understand the path of the sword, read your adversary's
mindset, and using various rhythms, attain victory in
any way. You must analyze this well.

The teaching of "position, no-position"

As for what is called "position, no-position", it means
that there shouldn't be such a thing as "taking a position"
with swords. However, since they can be placed
in five orientations, there should also be five

positions. But according to the adversary's approach, according to the place and following the circumstances, whatever position you place the swords in they are always held with the intention of being able to cut down the opponent easily.

The raised position, depending on the occasion, may have the feeling of being lowered somewhat, and become a "middle" position. The middle position, too, in accordance with principle may be moved up a little, and become a "raised" position. The lowered position as well, from time to time, if raised a little, becomes a "middle" position. The positions of both sides, if moved a little toward the centre, based on conditions, basically become "middle" or "lowered" positions.

Accordingly, there is the principle that "positions" both exist and do not exist.

Above all, when taking up swords, no matter how you hold them, it is with the intention of cutting down your opponent.

Even though there are things like parrying, blocking, hitting, sticking to or touching the opponent's sword, and so forth, you must understand that they are all for the purpose of cutting down the adversary. Think to parry, think to block, think to hit, or to stick, or to touch, and as a result your cutting will be insufficient.

To think of everything as a chance to cut [your opponent down] is crucial. Investigate this thoroughly.

In large-scale strategy, with numerous people, there are also "positions". There too, they are all a means of winning the battle.

[In any situation] to become settled or fixed is bad. Work this out diligently.

Striking the opponent in "one beat"

In the rhythms of striking an opponent, there is what is called "one beat". You grasp that you and your adversary are each in a position to hit the other, understand the moment when the opponent cannot react, and strike without moving your body and without attaching your mind to anything – this is an exceedingly quick and direct rhythm of striking.

The rhythm of hitting before the opponent can think to pull back his sword, move it out of the way, or strike: this is "one beat".

Learn this rhythm well and acquire it, and train to strike quickly in the beat of an interval.

The "rhythm of two advances"

The "rhythm of two advances":[16] when you go to strike and your opponent quickly pulls back or moves to block, you feign a strike; then when the adversary tries to parry or pull back again, strike him there. This is the "rhythm of two advances". Just by reading what is written here, it will be extremely difficult to grasp how to strike like this. However, if you are taught you will come to understand it very quickly.

Striking with "no thought, no form" [17]

When your adversary is about to strike, and you also want to strike, with your body becoming the body of the strike and your spirit becoming the spirit of striking, your hand spontaneously strikes out of nowhere, quickly and powerfully. This – called "no thought, no form" – is a strike of paramount importance. This strike is a frequently used one; learn it well, and train in it diligently.

"Flowing-water" striking

In what is called "flowing-water" striking, when you close with the enemy and your adversary tries to pull back quickly or disengage, or when he suddenly tries to knock your long sword aside, you expand both your body and your spirit, and with your long sword following after your body

– very smoothly, like water that has been dammed
up running over – strike broadly and powerfully.
Once you learn and understand this strike, it becomes
a very easy way to strike indeed.

It is vital to discern the bearing[18] of your opponent.

The "opportune" hit

When you strike, and your opponent tries to parry your
attack or knock it aside, strike at his head, hands and legs
all in one stroke, and in the path of your long sword,
strike anywhere – this is the "opportune strike".[19] Practise
and learn this strike well; it is a strike that can be employed
at any time. To understand the fine points, you need
to [use this technique when you] actually fight,
and analyze it.

The "flint-and-spark" blow

The "flint-and-spark" blow: your adversary's long sword and
your own are close enough to touch, and without raising

your sword even a little, you strike very powerfully. This is
done powerfully with the legs, powerfully with the body and
powerfully with the arms – you should strike quickly with all
three of these together. Unless you practise this strike many
times it is hard to do, but if you train well you will be able
to strike very hard [with it].

"Autumn-leaves" striking

In "autumn-leaves"[20] striking, you knock down the enemy's
sword and take it away. When your opponent takes up a
position in front of you and tries to strike, block or parry, if
you strike his long sword strongly in the spirit of either the
"no thought, no form" or "flint-and-spark" blow, and then
immediately strike it again with a feeling of knocking it
away, continuing your strike until your own sword-tip points
down, your opponent's sword will definitely fall. This strike,
if you train well, will make it easy to knock your adversary's
sword from his hand. You should practise this thoroughly.

The body replaces the sword

This could also be called "the sword replaces the body".
Generally, when striking an opponent, the sword and the

body do not strike at the same time. When the enemy comes within striking range, go in first with your body as if to strike with it, and the sword then strikes necessarily, without regard for the body. There are certain circumstances where the long sword strikes first without the body moving, but on the whole, the body moves in first and the sword strikes afterwards. You should investigate this deeply as you practise your striking.

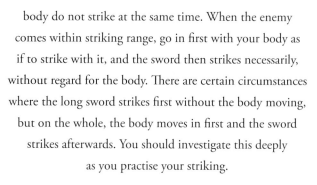

On "striking" and "hitting"

What is called "striking" and what is called "hitting" are two different things. The spirit of striking, no matter which type of strike is used, is that it is done with great resolution and certainty. As for hitting, if you go in with the intention of just hitting anything, even if you hit incredibly strongly and your opponent dies immediately, this is still "hitting". A strike is performed with intent. You should investigate this.

Whether you hit your adversary's arm or leg, in any case it is still just hitting. It only serves the purpose of allowing you to execute a strong strike afterwards. Hitting has the sense of being like touching.[21] If you practise well, you will be able to distinguish the two; you should work this out.

The "body of the autumn monkey" [22]

The "body of the autumn monkey" is about the feeling of not overextending the arms. When entering the opponent's space, with the feeling of not reaching out with your hands even a little, be intent on quickly getting your body in before you strike your adversary. [23]

If you think to reach out with your hands, your body will certainly stay far back, so you need to focus on quickly getting close with your body. If you are at a distance [24] where you can engage with your hands, you can easily get your body in. Test this out fully.

The "lacquer-glue" body

"Lacquer-glue" means when you get your body in and stick very tightly, intending not to separate. When you get right up next to your opponent's body, press with your face, press with your body, and press with your legs, very strongly.

Everyone tends to get in quickly with their face and feet,
but leaves their body back.
Stick your body to your opponent's body tightly, so as not
to allow even the slightest space between your bodies.
This is something that needs to be investigated well.

"Comparing heights"

In speaking of "comparing heights", this is how any time
you get in close with your opponent, you do not allow
your body to shrink – you extend your legs, extend your
torso, extend your neck and close in powerfully, getting
your face right up next to your adversary's. Think of
it like you are comparing heights, and proving that
you are the taller.[25]
It is crucial to extend yourself to your full height and move
in strongly. You should work on this extensively.

To become "sticky"

When the enemy attempts to strike, and you also go to
strike with your long sword, and the enemy intercepts it,
apply your sword to your opponent's with a feeling of
"stickiness" as you move in. "Stickiness" is just a feeling

of making it hard for the adversary's sword to get away;
don't try to put too much strength into it.

If you engage the enemy's sword and apply "stickiness",
when you close in you can do so as calmly as you please,
without difficulty.

There is what is called "stickiness", and there is what is called
"entanglement". "Stickiness" is strong; "entanglement"
is weak. You need to differentiate these things.

The "body hit"

A "body hit" is when you get up next to your opponent and
strike him with your body. You turn your face a little to the
side, stick out your left shoulder, and hit your opponent in
the chest. The hit is done as hard as possible, and it is done
suddenly, with a feeling of bouncing him away.

If you learn how to get "inside" like this, it is strong enough

that you can knock your adversary back two or three *ken*.[26]
It is also possible to hit the enemy hard enough to kill him.
You should train in this well.

Three parries

I talk about three parries:
At the time you close in on your opponent and
he strikes out with his long sword, to intercept it
make as if you were going to stab him in the eye
with your long sword, and deflect his sword by
pulling it past your right shoulder, parrying
it in this way.

Next, in what I call the "thrusting parry", receive your
opponent's sword by stabbing at his right eye, with a feeling
of scissoring his neck as you thrust at him.[27]

Or, when your adversary strikes, get inside his strike
with your short sword, without particularly worrying
about his sword, moving in and trying to thrust your
left hand into his face.

These are the three parries. Think of them like you are clenching your left [28] hand into a fist and punching your opponent in the face with it. This is something that you should train in very thoroughly.

"Stabbing the face"

This is what is meant by "stabbing the face": when you face your adversary, in between his sword-blows and yours, it is essential that you constantly remember to keep the feeling of stabbing him in the face with the tip of your sword.[29]

If you have the mindset of stabbing your opponent in the face, he will try to get both his face and his body out of the way, and when he tries to get away, you benefit from a variety of opportunities for victory. You need to work this out well. During battle, if the enemy's mind is on getting his body out of the way, you have already won.

For this reason you should never forget what I call "stabbing the face". Whenever you are practising strategy you should exercise this principle, and train in it.

"Stabbing the heart"

As for what is called "stabbing the heart", when in the midst of battle you are constrained, such as from above or at the side, so that it is difficult for you to cut in any way, you should thrust into your opponent. With the feeling of slipping the blow of his sword, show the back edge of your long sword straight to your adversary and – pulling it back without allowing the tip to twist – thrust it into your opponent's chest.

You can also get by using this technique alone, at times such as when you are very tired, or when your sword has become unable to cut. You need to discern this properly.

"Katsu-totsu"

As for *katsu-totsu*,[30] whenever you go to strike your adversary, when you move in to strike and your opponent tries to strike back at you, raise up [your sword] from below as if to stab the enemy with it, and turning it, strike coming back [down] – with an extremely fast rhythm, strike: *katsu-totsu*!

The feeling is that you raise it up with "*katsu*" and then strike with "*totsu*". This rhythm should be used whenever exchanging strikes. The way to do *katsu-totsu* is to go in with the feeling of raising the tip of yours sword, as if thinking to stab the opponent, and in the same beat as raising it, strike. You should test this out through extensive practice.

"Slapping deflection"

The "slapping deflection" is when you are exchanging blows with your adversary and it falls into a regular back-and-forth ("*totan-totan*") rhythm, you meet one of your opponent's blows by striking and slapping your long sword against his. The feeling of this should not be one of slapping very hard; neither is it "blocking". Anticipate the enemy's sword, swat it aside and immediately[31] strike your opponent. By slapping take the initiative, and by striking take the initiative – this is the crucial point.

If you time the slap well, no matter how hard your
adversary strikes, with a feeling of swatting it just a little
your sword point will not be knocked down.
You should learn this well and test it.

The "bearing for many opponents"

The "bearing for many opponents" is what we call it
when one person fights against a large group.
Drawing both your *katana* and *wakizashi*, take a position
with the swords out broadly to the left and right. Whichever
of the four directions opponents attack from, your aim is
to chase them around in one direction.

Determine the order in which your adversaries are
preparing to attack, and quickly go to meet whichever
one advances first, keeping your field of vision broad, and
when you grasp that an enemy is about to strike, swing both
the right and left swords [32] in opposite directions at once.
Waiting is bad.

Quickly return to a stance with the swords positioned
at both sides, and move in, cutting powerfully, where an
adversary advances and crush him; just like that, when again
an enemy advances, attack in that direction, and cut
him apart – that's the idea.

As much as possible, get your adversaries in one line and chase them around as if they were a school of fish.[33] If you see that they are piled up, immediately – without allowing a pause – cut into them powerfully.

If, when your enemies advance, you just keep chasing them around and around as a group, it is very hard to get anywhere. On the other hand, if you keep thinking about which direction each enemy is going to come from next, this is a mindset of waiting, and won't get you anywhere either.

Perceive your adversaries' rhythms and understand where they fall apart, and you will win.

If occasionally you get a large group of training partners together, engage with them, and grasp the heart of this, you will feel at ease whether you are against one opponent, ten or twenty. You should practise this well and investigate it.

The principles of combat

As for these principles of combat, they are a way of
understanding how to use strategy to achieve victory using
the sword. They are not to be written about in detail –
you have to learn to win by way of thorough practice.

Basically, the true Way of all Strategy is revealed through
the sword. (Oral tradition.)[34]

Just "one strike"

This "one strike", as it is called – if you have the spirit of it,
you are certain to gain victory.[35] It is very difficult to get this
without learning strategy thoroughly.

If you train diligently in this skill, you will get to the heart of
strategy itself, and in this way become able to win at will.
You must practise constantly.

"Direct transmission"

The heart of "direct transmission" is in receiving the true Way of the *Ni Tō Ichi Ryū* [Two Swords One Style] and passing it on. To train ever-diligently, and to embody this strategy, is vital. (Oral tradition.)[36]

What I have written above in this scroll is to record my style of sword technique in a very general way for the future.

As for strategy, in order to learn how to take swords and achieve victory over people: first, through the five standard forms, understand the five orientations of position, and learn the natural path of the sword. Your whole body will become pliable, your mind become very effective, and you will understand the rhythms of the Way.[37] Both you yourself and your sword technique will become sharp and clear. When your body and legs become able to move freely, just as you wish, you will beat one person, beat two people, and you will come to understand what is good and bad in strategy.

Practise what is in this writing point by point, and engage
in combat with various opponents, gradually acquiring
the principles of the Way. Set your mind to this ceaselessly,
without being in a rush; whenever you have a chance,
put your hand to the sword and learn its virtues. Engage in
combat with anyone and everyone, and learn their mindsets.

Even a path of a thousand *ri*[38] is walked one step at a time.
Do not hurry, but carry out this practice steadily,
remembering that it is the duty of a warrior.

Thinking, "today I will defeat who I was yesterday; tomorrow I will defeat the less skillful, and after that, I will defeat the more skilled", do as directed in these writings and resolve not to allow your heart to be sidetracked. No matter how many adversaries you may overcome, to turn your back on your training is not in the true Way.

When the fundamental principles appear [39] in your mind, you will understand the mindset that allows you to overcome tens of opponents alone. Having achieved that, you will realize [40] strategy on both the large and small scale.

Forge yourself with a thousand days of training, and polish yourself with ten thousand days of practice. This is something you need to investigate thoroughly.

Shōhō [Era] Second Year, Fifth Month, Twelfth Day
Shinmen Musashi
[to] Terao Magonojō

Kanbun [Era] Seventh Year,[41] Second Month, Fifth Day
Terao Yumeyo Katsunobu
[given to] Yamamoto Gennosuke [honorific][42]

FIRE

In the strategy of the *Ni Tō Ichi Ryū* [Two Swords One Style], I think of battle as being like fire, and so I consider battle and single combat in the "Fire" scroll, and write about these things in this scroll.

To start with, people of the world all think about the principles of strategy in a small way, whether it has something to do with the fingertips, knowing how to create an advantage of three *sun* or five *sun* [1] with the wrist, or else using a fan and trying to figure out how to win using the forearms, or with something like a bamboo sword, trying to learn to get an advantage from even a little bit of extra speed, trying to sharpen their handwork and footwork, and specializing in taking advantage of these small differences in speed.

In strategy, we risk our lives fighting many times in single combat, discern the principles of life and death, learn the path of the sword, understand the strengths and weaknesses of the opponent's sword, distinguish the paths of the blade and back edges of the sword, and train to be able to strike down our opponents. In this we cannot bother thinking about small things. Particularly when, for example, you are wearing armour, [2] there is no time to think about trivial points; moreover, when you are fighting for your life, alone, against five or even ten men, to understand with certainty the way to victory – that is our Way of Strategy. That being the case, whether one person is defeating ten, or if with a thousand men you are beating ten thousand – in the principles, what is the difference? You must investigate this well.

However, if you take up your swords alone, judge each
of your opponents' resources, and understand their strengths and
weaknesses, you will attain the wisdom and virtue of strategy,
and perfect the way to take victory against ten thousand; you
will have become a master of this Way.

Our correct Way of Strategy – who else in all the world
will grasp it or refine it so well? We must certainly wonder.
Training morning to night, once you have polished it to
perfection, you will achieve an independent freedom, naturally
also acquire wondrous abilities, and have mysterious, limitless
power. This is the spirit of the practice we undertake as warriors.

Circumstances of place

In discerning a place's bearing, there is what is called "shouldering
the sun". This means putting the sun at your back. If there is a
situation where you cannot keep the sun behind you, you should
try to keep it on your right side. When you are indoors as well,
keep the light behind you or to your right, as just mentioned
previously. Try not to allow yourself to be blocked to the rear,
keep space open to your left,[3] and keep your right closed off.
At night, so you can see your opponents, keep fires at your
back and light to your right when you position yourself.
You should position yourself keeping the above[4] in mind.

We also talk about "looking down on your opponent".
You should try to take a position that is slightly higher than
the surroundings. Indoors, think of the place of honour [5]
as being the high ground.

Then, once the battle begins, when you are chasing your
adversaries around, do so with the feeling of chasing them
to your left. It is essential to put difficult surroundings
behind your opponents, and in any situation try to drive
them into adverse terrain.

In awkward spots, we also say, "don't let your opponent see
the place": this means not to let your adversary look around,
and press him without giving him a moment's relief. Indoors
as well, when driving your opponent towards thresholds,
lintels, sliding doors, verandas or pillars, "not letting him
see the place" is the same.

Any time you pursue your opponent, do so towards
bad footing, or places where there are obstructions
to the sides. In any case, utilize the special virtues of the
place, and be certain to "take victory by location".

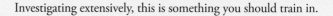

Investigating extensively, this is something you should train in.

The three kinds of initiative [6]

Of the three initiatives, one is when you take the initiative
first and launch an attack; this is called "advance initiative".
Another is the initiative you take when the opponent attacks
you first; this is called "waiting initiative". Still another is
when you attack and your adversary attacks at the same
time; this is called "simultaneous initiative". These are
the three kinds of initiative.

The beginning of any kind of battle never deviates from
these three types of initiative. Since the conditions of the
initiative can determine the victor from the outset, initiative
is the most important thing in strategy.

As for the details of these initiatives, of course they are
various. In each individual case you judge the appropriate
initiative, read your opponent's intention, and using the
wisdom and virtues of our style of strategy, take the victory;
there is no need to write out the particulars here.

Advance Initiative

First, advance initiative: when you think you want to
attack, stay calm, then suddenly attack with this initiative.
In this initiative, outwardly make yourself strong and fast,
but leave the depths of your mind still. Or, make your
spirit exceedingly strong, and walking a little faster than
usual, when you get close to your adversary, attack quickly
with this initiative. Alternatively, let go of your intentions,
and keeping this the same in the beginning, middle and
end, with the feeling of utterly dominating your adversary,
fill your spirit with strength to your very depths,
and win like that.

Waiting Initiative

Second, waiting initiative: when the adversary advances to
attack you, do not worry about it at all, and show your
opponent an appearance of weakness. When the opponent
draws near, boom![7] – suddenly become strong, and appear
as if you will jump at him; see when he slackens a little, and
immediately and strongly take the victory there. Another
thing you can do is when the opponent advances, advance
even more strongly and, seeing the openings in the changes
of his rhythm, quickly take the victory there. These are
types of waiting initiative.

Simultaneous Initiative

Third, simultaneous initiative. When the enemy
advances quickly, advance at him calmly but strongly,
and when he gets close – boom! – give it your all, and
when you see the slightest relaxation in the adversary, directly
and powerfully take the victory there. On the other hand,
when the adversary advances calmly, approach him
somewhat quickly, with a light, "floating" feeling.
As he nears, engage with him once to feel him
out, and adjusting your attack to his condition,
strike strongly and take the victory.

It is impossible to write out all these techniques in detail.
From these writings you must work out the rest. With these
three types of initiative, depending on the occasion and
according to principle, you may not always be the one to
attack first; however, just as when you do attack first,
you want to move the opponent around at will.

In any type of initiative, employing the wisdom of strategy,
be intent on winning no matter what. You must
train continuously.

"Holding the pillow down"

By "holding the pillow down" we mean the idea of
not allowing the adversary [even] to lift his head
[from his pillow].

Specifically in the Way of Strategy for single combat,
to let a person move you around and put you on the
defensive is bad. At all times, you want to move your
adversary around freely.

Of course, your opponent will be thinking this same thing.
As you have the same intention, it is very difficult
constantly to be adapting to what the other person does.
Thus in strategy we stop the opponent before he strikes,
hold him back before he thrusts, pull out before he can
grapple with you, and so forth.

"Holding the pillow down", once you have grasped the true
Way, is realizing whatever your opponent intends to do

when he comes to attack you, and not allowing him to
do it: stop the adversary's strike at the beginning "s",
and do not allow him to continue – this is the essence of
"holding the pillow down". Likewise, if the adversary thinks
to attack, hold him back at "a"; if he goes to jump, cut him
off at "j"; if he thinks to cut, restrain him at "c". These are
all done in the same spirit.

When your opponent attempts to use a technique against
you, allow him to do things which are useless; things which
will be useful, stop them before he has begun and do not
allow him to continue – this is one of the most important
things in strategy.

In this too, though, if you are constantly thinking "hold him
down, hold him down", you will end up on the defensive.
Basically, no matter what the situation, while entrusting your
techniques to the Way, when the adversary attempts to use a
technique [just] stop him at the thought; do not allow him
to do anything useful, and move him around at will. This is
the mark of a master strategist, and the result of extensive
training and practice.

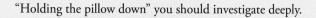

"Holding the pillow down" you should investigate deeply.

"Getting across"

We talk about "getting across": for example, in crossing the seas there are crossings at narrow straits, and there are also long crossings at channels of forty or fifty *ri*.[8] As you make your way through the human world as well, in the course of a lifetime there are many instances of "getting across".

Concerning sea voyages, you need to know the locations of these crossings, understand the capabilities of the boat, and take the weather well into consideration. Even without putting a pilot boat out, you must be able to adjust to the changes of the moment, sometimes using crosswinds, at other times taking tailwinds – or if the wind changes you may need to use the rudder-oar or put in pairs of oars for two or three *ri*; dead set on making port, you steer your ship, and in this way make the crossing.

Adopting this mindset while making your way through the world of people as well, when you reach an important event you should have the same determination to "get across".

In strategy, during battle, "getting across" is crucial. Adapting to the opponent's condition, understanding your own abilities, using principles to get through: this is just the same as a good ship's captain making a sea crossing. Once you have "got across", then you can relax again.

What we mean by talking about "getting across" is weakening the opponent, taking the initiative and essentially securing the victory in advance, right there. In both large- and small-scale strategy it is vital to have this spirit of "getting across". You should consider this deeply.

*Understanding
the situation*

"Seeing the situation", in large-scale strategy, means
perceiving the enemy's weakening or growing in power,
understanding the intentionsof the opponent's forces, getting
the lay of the land, discerning well the conditions of the
enemy, knowing how many of your own troops to deploy –
and to all of these applying the principles of strategy in such
a way as to ensure victory, know the condition of the
initiative, and in this way engage in battle.

In the strategy of single combat as well, to perceive the
opponent's style, to discern the adversary's strengths and
weaknesses, and his character, to do things which go counter
to his manner, to understand his modulations and, grasping
well the intervals and rhythms therein, take the initiative –
all this is vital.

In all things, if your wisdom is powerful, you will absolutely
be able to see the situation.

When through strategy you become a creature of total freedom, you will be able to assess your opponent's mindset well, and this will be something that provides you with many ways to win. You must work this out.

"Stomping down the sword" [9]

The idea of "stomping down the sword" has a very specialized meaning in strategy. First of all, in large-scale strategy, where bows or guns are concerned, when the enemy fires in your direction with whatever it is they have, and you try to attack them *after* they have released their shots, they immediately nock their bows and pack their rifles with powder again, so it is difficult to charge them anew.

When dealing with bows or guns, the key is to strike quickly while the enemy is in the middle of firing. If you attack swiftly, it is difficult to nock arrows, and there is little chance to fire a gun, either. Each thing the enemy tries to do,

immediately perceive the principle to be employed against it, and win by stomping down everything the enemy does.

Likewise, in individual strategy, if you strike after your adversary strikes out at you, you get into a back-and-forth ("*totan-totan*"), and it becomes impossible to advance. Instead, strike him with the feeling of stomping down his sword as he strikes out and beat him right at his strike; make it such that he doesn't get a second chance to attack.

What is called "stomping" is not limited to the feet. Stomp with your whole body, stomp with your spirit, and of course stomp with your sword, determined not to let your adversary make a second attack. This, in other words, means being intent on taking the initiative in any situation. It does not mean running directly into your opponent at the same time as he attacks; it is getting on him immediately after he does so. You need to investigate this carefully.

Understanding collapse

"Collapse" is something that is inherent in all things. The

collapse of a given house, the collapse of a person's body and also the collapse of an enemy [army]: when the time comes, their rhythms become disrupted and they collapse.

In large-scale strategy also, to perceive the collapse of the enemy's rhythm, and to run them down without allowing that moment to slip away, is essential. If you let the moment of collapse go by, they have the chance to recover.

Likewise in strategy for single combat, in the midst of fighting, when your adversary's rhythms are thrown off, strike at the point where he begins to collapse. If you slack off and let it go by, he can recover and renew his attack, and you will not be able to advance. It is crucial to attack that initial crumbling and, so that the opponent cannot raise his face again, to decisively chase him down at this point.

Chasing down should be done directly and powerfully; you need to smash the enemy to bits, so that he cannot recover. You should carefully analyze what I call "smashing to bits". If you do not smash [the enemy] to bits, a tenaciousness will remain [in him]. This is something you need to work out.

火

Becoming the adversary

"Becoming the adversary" means you should think of yourself in the place of your opponent. Looking around the world, you see people who have committed a robbery or some such, and they hole themselves up in a house; they are thought of as being

an adversary in a position of strength. However, if you put yourself in that opponent's place, with everyone in the world against him, on the run – he feels desperate, perhaps hopeless.

The person who holes himself up is the pheasant,
the one who goes in to cut him down is the hawk.
You need to work this out thoroughly.

In large-scale strategy as well, if you convince yourself that the enemy is strong, you will think it a very serious matter to attack them. However, if you always have good soldiers, understand thoroughly the deep principles of strategy and know without a doubt that you will beat the enemy, there is nothing in your path to worry about at all.

Likewise, in individual strategy, you should
imagine yourself as your opponent. Understand
strategy well; your mastery of the deep principles of the
Way will be strongly evident, and anyone encountering
a person who has mastered the Way like this will
believe that he will certainly lose. You should
reflect seriously on this.

Releasing "four hands" [10]

Releasing "four hands" is for when both you and your
opponent have the same intent, and there is a feeling that
you are just struggling against one another – you cannot
advance in the battle like this. If you think that you are
about to become deadlocked, immediately abandon your
previous intention, and using some other tactic of advantage,
figure out how to win.

In large-scale strategy, if you have the feeling that you
are reaching a "four-hands" impasse, you will be unable
to advance, and will just wear out or lose many of your
people. Quickly abandon your plan, and attain victory
by using a tactic your enemy does not expect –
this is extremely important.

Similarly, in individual combat, if you think you are going to get into a "four-hands" deadlock, immediately change your approach – it is vital to perfect how to gauge your opponent's attitude and use a completely different tactic to win. You need to investigate this carefully.

"*Moving the shadows*" [11]

What we call "moving the shadows" is something for occasions when we are unable to understand our opponent's intention clearly.

In strategy on the large scale, when you cannot discern the enemy's situation at all, present as if you are going to attack powerfully, and you will see the enemy's intention. Having seen their approach, it will be easy to win by taking a different tactic.

Likewise, in one-on-one situations when your adversary takes a position such as with his sword behind him

or to his side,[12] if you suddenly make as if to strike, what your adversary is thinking will be revealed in [what he does with] his sword. When that has been revealed and understood, immediately perceive where your advantage lies; at this point you should certainly be able to assess how to achieve victory. [However,] if you allow your vigilance to slacken, the beat [13] will slip by. You should assess this carefully.

火

"Stifling the form" [14]

As for what is called "stifling the form", this is something used when we see the intention of the enemy to attack.

In large-scale strategy, at the point when the adversary is about to engage a tactic, you "stifle" it – if, just as you suppress the gambit, you show your full force to the enemy, they will be inhibited by that strength, and the opponent will change their approach. You then also alter your approach, and from an "empty" mindset (*kū naru kokoro yori*)[15] take the initiative, and victory.

Similarly in single combat, when the opponent gives
the strong feeling of being about to attack, make him
stop by means of an advantageous rhythm[16], and in
the beat when he halts, perceive the opportunity
for victory and take the initiative.
You must work through this diligently.

Causing "contagion"

What is called "contagion" exists in various things. For
example, things like sleepiness are transmitted, and things
like yawning are catching as well. Timing, also, is infectious.

In large-scale strategy, when you can see that the enemy is
bustling about hurriedly doing things, do not allow your
side to be bothered in the slightest; if you show the enemy
that you are extremely relaxed, the enemy will be infected
with this from your side, and their will to attack will slacken.
When you think that this "infection" has occurred,
from an "empty" mindset[17] attack swiftly and powerfully
and you will achieve victory.

In the strategy of single combat as well, make your body and your mind relaxed, and when you perceive the moment that your adversary is slackening, strongly and quickly take the initiative and attack, gaining victory there – this is very important. Alternately, speaking of ways to weaken [the opponent], there are some [other] things that resemble this: one is a spirit of boredom, another is one of aimlessness, and yet another is a feeling of becoming weak.

You should work on these diligently.

Upsetting the opponent

What we mean by "upset" is in all kinds of things. One is the feeling of being in immediate danger. Second, there is the feeling of frustration.[18] Third is the feeling of being surprised by something unforeseen. You should study these well.

In large-scale strategy, "upsetting" is crucial. When the enemy least expects it, attack in such a way that they can't even take a breath, and before they have got their wits back about them, use your advantage, take the initiative and win. This is essential.

In individual strategy too: feign being very relaxed at first, then all of a sudden powerfully attack; following the vacillation of the adversary's mindset, and its effects, and without letting him take a breath, immediately perceive the advantage. It is vital to discern how to win in this way; you must examine this very well.

Menacing

What we call "menace" can be found in all kinds of things.
One feels frightened by something one never expected
to happen.

It is of the utmost importance, in large-scale strategy,
to instil fear in the enemy. For example, you can menace
with the sound of things, and you can menace by [suddenly]
making small things large.[19] Or you can menace by
abruptly appearing at the enemy's flank. These are all
times when fear is felt.
Grasping the rhythms of this fear, and using this advantage,
you should gain victory.

In the strategy of single combat also, it is vital to menace
with your body, menace with your swords and menace
with your voice – things that your adversary does not
expect, suddenly do, and perceiving the moment of his
fear, immediately gain victory. You should test this
out thoroughly.

"Mixing in" [20]

This is what is called "mixing in": when you and the enemy draw near and you both clash strongly, if you see that you are not making any progress, immediately mix in together as one with the enemy. While you are mixed in with the enemy, it is essential to use the advantage in that and gain victory.

Whether in large- or small-scale strategy, if you separate clearly between the opponent and yourself, and you are both intent on clashing against each other, this will not result in victory. When this happens, it is important to immediately mix in with the opponent, so that one cannot be distinguished from the other – grasp the virtue in that situation, understand how to win in those conditions and powerfully gain victory. You must investigate this well.

"Damaging the corners"

We talk about "damaging[21] the corners" – with various things, when you push against something

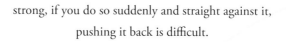

strong, if you do so suddenly and straight against it,
pushing it back is difficult.

In large-scale strategy, surveying the enemy's forces, attack
the "corners" of the sections that strike out strongly, and you
will gain some advantage. As one corner falters, the whole
will weaken as a result. It is essential that during this
faltering you keep going after [the enemy's] various
"corners", gaining the advantage that leads to victory.

Also in single-combat strategy, you should make injuries to
the "corners" of your opponent's body; when his body
becomes even a little weak, and takes on a collapsing[22] form,
it will be very easy to defeat him.

To test these things well, and to discern how to achieve
victory with them, is supremely important.

Unsettling

When I speak of "unsettling", this means not allowing
the adversary to keep a steady mindset.

In large-scale strategy, on the field of battle, gauge the spirit of your enemy, and using the wisdom of our style of strategy, disturb the enemy's mind so they do not know whether they are here or there; make them wonder whether to do this or that, and make them think they should go slower or faster. Grasp the rhythm of the adversary's unsettled mind, and determine how to take certain victory.

In strategy for individual combat as well, depending on the instance, attack with various techniques – make as if to strike, or feign a thrust, or make the opponent think you are about to charge in. When you perceive the signs that the opponent has become unsettled, you can defeat him freely; this is of the essence in combat. You must investigate this well.

The "three cries" [23]

As regards the "three cries", when we speak of these, there are shouts at the beginning, in the middle and after – we distinguish these three. It is necessary to apply the shouts according to the situation.

Since the voice has a vital force, we cry out when there is
a fire, and also cry out in the wind and waves; we cry out
to show our power.

Also in large-scale strategy – your cries at the beginning of
battle should be as loud as possible, so as to overwhelm the
enemy. Then, as for the voice used during battle: make
the tone lower, and attack with a voice from your very
depths. After you have won, cry out with a loud, strong
shout. These are the three cries.

Next, in single combat too: in order to move your opponent,
make as if to strike, shouting "*Ei!*" at the outset. Strike out
with your sword after the cry. Finally, after you have struck
down your opponent, you give a yell – this is a cry
to indicate your victory.

These are what we call "before and after" cries –
there is no shouting loudly at the same time as
[you swing] the sword. If you use your voice in the

middle of combat, your voice is timed with
your rhythm, and low.

You must examine this deeply.

"Cutting through waves" [24]

We talk about "cutting through waves" in large-scale strategy
when, as the forces engage, the enemy is strong and you attack
the opponent with the sense of "cutting through waves" – first
at one side, and when you see the enemy's forces crumble
there, abandon that, and attack another strong side.
Basically, to attack in a zigzag pattern [25] is the main idea.

In individual strategy, this idea is extremely important when you are confronted with many adversaries. Attack in different directions, and when [the enemies] flee in those directions, turn again to attack another strong opponent. Grasping the rhythms of the adversaries, and establishing a good rhythm [for yourself], go left and right: remember the feeling of zigzagging, keep an eye on your enemies' condition, and attack them [like that].

Understand your adversary's situation, and as you go forth striking, the principle is to take the victory powerfully, without even the slightest feeling of retreat.

When getting "inside" a single opponent as well, against a strong adversary there is the same feeling.

What is called "cutting through waves" means retreating even a single step is unthinkable. You must analyze the idea of "cutting through waves" very carefully.

Crushing

"Crushing" means, for example, viewing your opponent as weak and filling yourself with confidence – this feeling of "crushing" is very important.

In large-scale strategy, when you observe that the enemy has a small number of personnel, or even if they are a large force, when they are disorganized and you find their weak spots, what is called "crushing" means the idea that from the top down you dominate them totally and smash them.

If your "crushing" is weak, it is possible for them to rally.
The feeling should be like you are crushing them in your
hand – you need to understand this well.

Also, in times of individual strategy, when you encounter
someone unskilled, or when your opponent's rhythm is
thrown off and he seems like he is going to retreat, without
giving him even the slightest chance to breathe, and without
looking him in the eyes, crush him directly – this is essential.
The most important thing is not to give even the smallest
chance to recover. Investigate this well.

"Exchanging the mountain and sea"

The meaning of "exchanging the mountain and sea"
is that in the midst of battle with the enemy, doing the
same thing again and again is bad. Having to do the
same thing twice may be unavoidable, but you should
never do it three times.

When you employ a technique against an opponent, and
the first time it is unsuccessful, you can try it again, but if
it is ineffective then suddenly do something totally different.
If that does not get you anywhere, you should again attack
with something utterly different.

Thus, the heart of this is when the opponent is thinking
"mountain", attack with "sea"; if he thinks "sea", attack with
"mountain" – that is the Way of Strategy. This is something
you must examine thoroughly.

"Pulling the bottom out"

I call it "pulling the bottom out": what you should do when
you and an adversary are in battle, [you are] using the
principles of the Way [of Strategy], and it appears on the
surface that you have won, but at heart your opponent has
not given up – superficially he has lost, but at the bottom
of his heart he has not. This is something that happens.

On these occasions, abruptly change your approach –
extinguish your opponent's spirit, ripping out his heart from

the bottom, and observe that he knows he has completely lost; this is important. This "pulling the bottom out" you can do with the sword, or you can do with your body; you can even do it with your spirit. You cannot understand how to do this just in passing, though.

Once your adversary has collapsed to his very depths, there is no need for your attention to remain on him any further. Otherwise, though, you have to stay vigilant, and if you have to keep your attention [on him], it is hard to cause your enemy to collapse.

In both large-scale strategy and small, you should train thoroughly in "pulling the bottom out".

"Becoming new"

What we call "becoming new" is when you have the feeling that you and your opponent have become entangled and you cannot get anywhere, you shake off that feeling and start again with the feeling of everything becoming new; grasp that [new] rhythm, and understand how to take victory.

"Becoming new" is a thing you can do any time you realize you and your adversary have got into the feeling of just scraping along – you should immediately change your spirit, and employ a totally different tactic to win.

In large-scale strategy as well, it is vital that you understand what we call "becoming new". When you have the wisdom of strategy, you will be able to see it instantly. You should consider this deeply.

"Mouse's head–horse's neck" [26]

As for what is called "mouse's head–horse's neck", in the midst of combat with an adversary, when you both have gotten focused on particulars and are getting the feeling of being tangled up, remember that the Way of Strategy is always "mouse's head–horse's neck, mouse's head–horse's neck": [27] when things have become extremely minute, abruptly make your spirit very big; changing large and small is one of the fundamental ideas of strategy.

A person's usual mindset as well should be to think
"mouse's head–horse's neck"; it is the essence of a warrior.

In strategy, be it large-scale or small-scale, you should always
have this mindset. This is a thing you should examine fully.

"The general knowing his troops"

"The general knowing his troops" is how you engage in
any battle once you have achieved the Way [28] you have
set out on, ceaselessly carried out this practice, and grasped
the wisdom of strategy: you think of everyone who is
your adversary, all of them, as being your own troops.
You realize in your heart that you can make them do
as you want, and understand that you can move them
around freely – you are the general; your adversaries
are your troops. It is necessary to work this out.

"Releasing hold of the hilt"

When we say "releasing hold of the hilt", this is something that has various meanings. There is the idea of winning with no sword, and on the other hand there is the idea that [sometimes] you cannot win with the sword. The extent of the various different senses is such that they cannot all be written here. You must train extensively.

"The body of a massive rock"

What we call "the body of a massive rock" is when, having comprehended the Way of Strategy, you can suddenly become like a huge boulder: not one thing in ten thousand can hit you, nor can any move you. (Oral tradition.)[29]

Afterword

What I have written above about my style of swordsmanship I have considered ceaselessly, and decided to put these thoughts down in writing. Now I am recording these principles for the first time, and in writing them I feel I have mixed up the order, putting last things first, and it has been difficult to explain things in detail. However, for those people who want to learn this Way, these [writings] should serve as signposts for their minds.

Ever since my youthful years, I have set my heart on the Way of Strategy, and basically dedicated myself to the study of swordsmanship, training my hands and my body exhaustively, and taking on all manner of mindsets. I have gone out and seen the various other styles, but they were all either just full of pretentious talk, or concerned with elaborate hand techniques. Although they showed off in a way that looked impressive, not one of them had the true spirit. Of course, if you learn something like this, thinking to make your body effective, or to make your mind sharp, all of these just become obstructions to the Way, and are hard to get rid of, even much later. Thus the true Way of Strategy decays in the world, and for this reason the Way is abandoned.

Swordsmanship, if it is the true Way, is in engaging in combat with opponents and winning; this practice should not be altered at all.[30] If you grasp the wisdom of my strategy, and put it into practice correctly, it is unquestionable that you will win.

WIND

In strategy, it is important to understand the ways of other styles. Therefore I write about the various other styles as the scroll of "Wind", and record these things in this scroll. If you do not know the ways of other styles, it is certainly difficult to understand the Way of our style [and how it is different].[1]

Exploring other schools of strategy, we see that there are some styles that use extremely large swords, and emphasize physical strength to carry out their techniques. Conversely there are those styles that call themselves "short sword" (*kodachi*) schools, and use very small swords to train in their way. Then there are styles that contrive myriad techniques and positions of the sword, calling some of them "outer" (*omote*) and others "inner" (*oku*), and which teach their ways like this. None of these is the true Way.

In this scroll I will write all this out clearly, explaining the good and the bad, that which follows natural principles and that which diverges from them.[2] The Way and principles of my style are something totally different.

These other styles embellish and elaborate the fighting arts, rendering them flowery solely with the intention of making a living. Because they are fabrications, made up to be sold, how can they possibly be the true Way?

What is more, most people see strategy from a narrow perspective, thinking of it only as swordsmanship – [just] learning to swing a sword, to move their bodies effectively or concentrating on how to control their hands: have they truly understood how to achieve victory?

Of all of these, none is a Way with any certainty.

The other styles' shortcomings I will record in these writings. Investigating deeply, you should understand the advantages of the *Ni Tō Ichi Ryū* [Two Swords One Style].

Carrying a very long sword in other styles

There are styles other than ours [the *Ni Tō/Ni Ten Ichi Ryū*], which have a preference for a very long sword. From the perspective of my style of strategy, I view this as a weak style.

The reason for this is that these other styles of strategy, as they do not understand the principles that will allow them to beat a person no matter what the conditions are, think of the length of the sword as a virtue, and that it will allow them to beat an enemy from a distance; this must be the essence of why they prefer a very long sword.

Many people say "one *sun* of reach counts,"[3] but this is the talk of those who do not understand strategy. Accordingly, because they do not grasp the principles of strategy, they take something long and try to win from far away. This is evidence of a weakness of heart, and thus should be viewed as weak strategy.

If the enemy is in close – that is, near enough to grapple with – then the longer your sword is, the harder it is to strike with it. The sword becomes useless, or even gets in the way, and you are worse off than someone with only a short sword (*wakizashi*), or even someone unarmed.

As for people who prefer a very long sword, there are various explanations, but all are just those people's individual rationales. When viewed from the perspective of the true Way, out in the [real] world there is no reason for this preference. Not carrying a long sword at all, will someone with a short sword definitely lose? Also, in situations where one is blocked off above, below, at the sides, or some such, or when seated and one can only wear the *wakizashi*,[4] a strong preference for the long sword is in such cases strategically questionable, and thus a bad idea.

Some people are physically weaker, and for those who are so, sticking a long *katana* [through their belt] just does not work.

Since long ago, it has been said that "the large will answer to the small", but this does not mean to thoughtlessly avoid the long. It means you should avoid a feeling of *dependency* on the long.

In large-scale strategy, the very long sword is a large number of people; the short is a small number of people. A small number of people and a large one: do they not meet in combat? To win with a small number of troops – this, in fact, is the virtue of strategy. In the past as well, there are many examples where a small force took the victory from a large one.

In our style, these kinds of biased and narrow-minded ideas [above] are something to be avoided. You need to study this carefully.

Regarding other styles' use of a "forceful sword"

In swords, there should not be anything you call a "strong sword" or a "weak sword". Trying to swing the sword hard is a bad thing; winning with such rough techniques is difficult. Also, when you go to cut a person down, if you try to cut excessively strongly, calling it a "forceful sword", you will not be able to cut at all. Even when you just intend to cut test objects and the like,[5] if you try to cut forcefully, it is bad.

No matter who it is, no one, when he comes to sword-blows with an enemy, thinks to cut weakly, or to cut strongly. When you think about cutting a person down and killing him you do not intend to cut strongly, and of course you do not intend to cut weakly. The only thing you think is "enough for the enemy to die".

Also, with a "forceful sword", if you try to knock the other person's sword aside excessively strongly, you will overextend yourself, and this is always bad. If you hit someone else's sword very forcefully, it can happen that your own sword breaks apart, as well.

For these reasons, things like what is called a "forceful sword" and such do not exist [in our style].

In large-scale strategy as well, even when you have a strong number of troops, if you intend to win through sheer force when you engage in battle, the enemy also has strong troops and intends to fight hard as well. This is the same thing for both of you.

As for winning: in all things, if you abandon the principles of the Way, you will not win. In our Way, we do not think of forcing anything even a little; having the wisdom of strategy, the heart of it is to understand how to win in any way at all. You should work through this carefully.

The use of a much shorter sword in other styles

To think of winning by using very short swords exclusively is not the true Way.

Since long ago, [the uses of both] the long and the short [swords] have been clearly explained, calling them *tachi* and *katana*.

In the world, there are people of great strength, who can wield a very large sword as if it were quite light, so forcing oneself to prefer something short makes no sense, because these people can use long swords, as well as carry spears and *naginata*.[6]

Taking a short sword and trying to cut a person in the intervals between his swings of the long sword, or trying to jump in, trying to grab him and so forth – to rely on ideas like these is bad. Furthermore, looking for openings to attack is essentially to be seen as being on the defensive against everything; it has the feeling of becoming entangled, and is something to be avoided. If, using something small, you try to get in on your opponent and grapple with him or disarm him – when you are among many opponents this idea is not useful.

One who has become specialized in the use of the short [weapons] thinks to parry the cuts of many attackers, freely jump about and spin around, but all of these actions become what is called the "receiving sword", and have a feeling of being rushed. They are not a decisive way to do things.

In this kind of situation, it is better to make your body straight and strong, chase people around, make *them* jump away, and attack them in such a way that it drives them into a state of confusion – this is a way to assure certain victory.

In large-scale strategy, the same principle applies. In a similar situation, gather your forces, intending to press the enemy, drive into them fiercely, and immediately crush them. This is a key idea of strategy.

Most people, when learning to do these things, learn to parry, dodge, escape, duck and so forth; their minds become distracted by this way of doing things, and they are easily manipulated by other people.

The Way of Strategy is straight and true. Thus, having the correct principles, to drive people around and to cause them to do as you want is vital. You must study this deeply.

Very numerous sword techniques in other styles

Devising a great number of sword techniques and teaching them to people is just a technique for turning the Way into a commodity and selling it to them, with the intention of making beginners think that when they have learned a great number of techniques, they have understood deeply. This way of thinking about strategy is to be avoided.

The reason for this is that when you think about all the various ways there are to cut a person down, you can get the feeling of becoming lost. In fact, when it comes to cutting a person down, there is no "special way" to do it. Whether someone is knowledgeable [of swordsmanship] or ignorant, or even if you are a woman or a child: striking, chopping, slicing – there are not so many ways to do these things. As for anything different, you can talk about stabbing or "reaping", but other than those, there is nothing else. The way to do it is just to cut first, so there is no reason to have numerous detailed techniques.

However, depending on the place and conditions, it may happen that there are times when you are blocked in at the top, from the side, or the like; since it is true that you may not be able to hold your sword in a certain way, we have five forms, one for each of the five orientations.[7] Adding other than these – corkscrewing the hands, twisting the body, jumping, dodging – as ways of cutting a person down is not the true Way.

When cutting a person down, if you corkscrew your hands you cannot cut. If you twist your body you cannot cut. If you jump you cannot cut. If you dodge you cannot cut. None of these things is of any use at all.

In my style of strategy, you make your posture and your spirit straight; it is your adversary you make warp and bend, and you take victory by making your opponent's spirit twist and turn – this is vital. You should investigate this diligently.[8]

Other styles' use of special sword positions

Emphasizing special positions of the sword is a mistake. The only time in the world there would ever be "positions" is when there is not actually an adversary [in front of you].

These specifics are [like] taking general customs from long ago, making them the rules of today, and codifying them into laws. This has no place in the Way of single combat (*shōbu no michi*).[9] [Rather,] you must think of putting your opponent in a bad situation.

In all things, "taking a position" means trying to make use of immobility. Whether it is taking up a position in a castle, or whether it is making formations with the ranks and suchlike, the intent is to be strongly unmoving even when attacked by someone: this is the usual meaning.

As for the Way of strategy and single combat (*hyōhō shōbu no michi*), in all things you must be constantly intent on taking the initiative, always taking the initiative. The idea of "taking up a position" means waiting for someone else to take the initiative. You should work this out thoroughly.[10]

The Way of strategy and single combat lies in causing other people to move their positions, doing things the opponent has not imagined, or confounding the enemy, or upsetting him, or menacing him, and grasping the rhythm of when the adversary has become confused. In order to win, you must avoid defensive ideas like "taking a position".[11]

It is because of all this that in our Way we say "position, no-position", by which it is meant that even though we may happen to arrive in a certain position, we are not "taking up a position".

In large-scale strategy as well, understand the number of the enemy's forces, perceive the nature of the battlefield, know the condition of your own numbers, grasp their virtues, assemble your people and begin the battle; these are the essentials of engaging in combat. From having someone else take the initiative against you, to when you take the initiative – there is a twofold change [in your advantage].

Thinking to position your sword well and parry or deflect the adversary's sword skillfully is the same as taking spears and *naginata* and making a fence out of them, and then, when striking the enemy, pulling up the fence posts and using them again as spears and *naginata*. You should consider this deeply.

Setting the gaze in other styles

Among certain styles [of swordsmanship/strategy],
when they speak of "setting the gaze", there are those that
fix the gaze on the opponent's sword, and styles that fix
the gaze at the hands. There are also those that fix the
gaze on the face, or set the gaze on the feet, and so on.
Separating things into parts and trying to fix the gaze
on them like this is a distraction to the mind, and is to
be regarded as a blight on strategy.

An example of this is players of *kemari*,[12] who despite not
looking closely at the ball, can kick *binzuri*.[13] Even rolling
off *ohimari*,[14] or spin-kicking: they are accustomed to
kicking, so there is no need to look closely with the eyes.

Or, for example, the techniques of people who do acrobatics
and so forth: when they have become used to their Ways,
even when perching doors on the tips of their noses, juggling
any number of swords and such, none of them sets their gaze
fixedly on anything, but since they are accustomed to what
they are doing, they see "naturally".

In the Way of Strategy as well, when you are accustomed
to facing opponents, you will be able to see the lightness or
heaviness of their minds; when you have practised and grasped
the Way, you will also be able to see the distance and speed
of any sword.

The gaze in strategy, broadly, is an eye that rests upon the
other person's mind (*kokoro*).

In strategy on the large scale as well, it is the eye that rests
upon the condition of the enemy's forces.

There are two ways of viewing: perceiving and looking.
Make the perceiving eye strong, see that particular opponent's
mind, and see the conditions of that place. Setting the gaze
broadly, see the circumstances of the battle, see the changes of
power in that particular moment, and secure [15] certain victory;
that is the essence.

In either large-scale strategy or small, there is no fixing the gaze minutely. As I have written before, if you set your view closely on particulars, you forget about large things; the feeling arises of your view becoming lost, and certain victory slips away from you.

Carefully investigate these principles, and train in them.

The use of the feet in other styles

The ways of stepping with the feet [in other styles] include those that are called "floating" feet, "flying" feet, "bouncing" feet, "creeping" feet, and "crow" feet; there are various specialized manners of treading. All of them, viewed from the perspective of my strategy, are to be considered lacking.[16]

As for avoiding "floating" feet, the reason for this is that when it comes to battle, your feet will always want to "float", and thus the way to do it is to be sure to tread as firmly as possible.

Next, you should not develop a liking for "flying" feet. In "flying" feet, when you jump there is a beginning,[17]

and when you land there is a feeling of fixedness; [18] there cannot be said to be any advantage in jumping around again and again, so "flying" feet are bad.

Then there are "bouncing" feet. [19] With the feeling of "bouncing" you will not be able to advance.

As for "creeping" feet, [20] they are "waiting feet", and as such they are something to be particularly avoided.

Besides these, there are "crow" feet, various kinds of quick-stepping, and so forth.

When you are in a swamp, or on a moor, or else when you are on a mountain, in a river, in a stony field, or on a narrow path, and you cross swords with an opponent, there are situations where you cannot jump around, and cannot step quickly.

太平記英勇傳 笹井久藏尚信

In our strategy, nothing is changed about the feet.
It is just like walking down the street as usual.
You should move in accordance with the opponent's
rhythm, when moving quickly maintaining the same
demeanour and posture as when you move slowly,
not moving too little or too much, and without
disorder in your steps.

In large-scale strategy, the carrying of the feet is crucial.
The reason for this is that if, not knowing the enemy's intent,
you recklessly attack quickly, you go against the [natural]
rhythm [of the battle] and it is difficult to win.

Conversely, if you tread [too] slowly, you may miss seeing
a point when the enemy wavers and begins to collapse,
and let a chance for victory slip away, and so you
cannot finish the battle quickly.

When you discern a moment of disruption and collapse,
it is essential to take the victory without allowing the enemy
to have even the slightest pause to recoup. You should train
and practise this thoroughly.

The use of speed in other schools of strategy

A strategy of "being fast" is not the true Way. What is called "being fast" is, in all things, not being coordinated with the intervals of their rhythms; thus things are said to be "fast" or "slow". When you become skilled in this Way, you do not appear to be fast. For example, there are people called "express couriers" (*haya-michi*), who can cover forty or fifty *ri*[21] in a day. They do not run fast from morning to night, either. Unseasoned runners, even if they run all day long, do not make much progress.

In the Way of Noh drama, when a good singer chants a piece, if a less-skilled performer chants along with him, there is the feeling that he is falling behind, and rushing to catch up. Or, when beating the drum for "The Old Pine" (*Oimatsu*),[22] although it has a slow tempo, an unskilled drummer similarly will lag behind, and try to jump ahead. As for "High Sands" (*Takasago*),[23] it has a quick pace, but it is bad to play it "fast". "He who hurries, falls," as they say, "and winds up late."[24] Of course, being too slow is also bad.

When skilled people do something, they may appear to move quite slowly, but they never miss a beat. In anything, when trained people do it, they never appear to be rushed. Taking these examples, you should understand the principles of the Way.

Especially in the Way of Strategy, trying to "go fast" is bad. The reason for this, too, is that depending on the place, such as in swamps and moors, it is difficult to move quickly, for both the feet and the body. As for the sword, cutting quickly is bad. If you try to cut fast, since it is not like a fan[25] or a knife, cutting with it quickly you will not be able to cut even a little. You must learn to discern this well.

In large-scale strategy as well, a feeling of rushing quickly is bad. If you keep the intention of "holding the pillow down", you will never be even a little slow. Furthermore, in situations where a person is being excessively fast, it is essential for you to "go contrary": become slow and calm, and do not be drawn in. The spirit of this is something you must work out, train, and practise.

"Deep" and "surface" teachings in other styles

Regarding the points of strategy, which should be called "surface" and which called "deep"? In the arts, each of them has what are called things like "secret teachings of deepest meaning" or "deep" [teachings] and "entrance" [teachings], but in the principles for times when you enter into combat with an opponent, it is not like you go into battle with "surface" [teachings] and cut someone down using "deep".

As for how to teach my strategy: with people who are just beginning to learn the Way, first have them practise those techniques that are easy to get used to, and teach them those principles that are quickly appreciated. For things that are difficult to understand,[26] you should discern the points at which that person's mind frees up,[27] and gradually teach the deeper principles.

However, in general, since you are getting them to learn things that depend on the situation, there aren't any such things as "deep" or "entrance" [teachings].

You know, out in the world, if you go walking "deep" in the

mountains, if you think to go as deep as possible into them, instead you eventually come out at an "entrance".[28]

In the Way of any given thing, there are situations where "deep" teachings are applicable, and cases in which using "entrance" principles is more appropriate.

In this Way of Battle,[29] though, what is to be hidden, and what to be revealed? [There is no difference between "deep" and "surface" teachings.] For this reason, in transmitting our Way, I have no liking for things such as oaths of secrecy.

Assess the intelligence of those people who learn this Way [of the *Ni Ten Ichi Ryū*], and teach them the correct Way, which will cause them to leave behind the bad points of the Five Ways/Six Ways[30] found in strategy. Then, naturally, they will enter the true way of the warrior's practice, and develop a heart free of doubt – this is how to teach my strategy.

You must train thoroughly.

Afterword

Above, I have set out nine articles regarding the other schools of strategy, and written them down in this scroll of "Wind". I probably should have written about them specifically, one by one, each school, from "entrance" to "deep" teachings, but I deliberately have not said what was important for which style or indicated them by name. The reason for this is that even if I individually pointed out each style and had my say on each of their ways, each person, following his own mind, has his own individual way of thinking; even within the same style, the ideas change little by little. Then later I would continually have had to write periodic updates for each style.

The general ideas of the other styles I have divided into these nine sections: if you look around at the techniques of the people in the world at large, some are biased towards long [weapons], some say the shorter are advantageous, some are biased towards using "strong", or "rough", or "precise" techniques. All these are prejudiced ways of doing things, and so without going into everything from the "entrance" to the "deep" [teachings] of the other styles, everyone should understand [what I am talking about].

In my style, the sword has neither "depths" nor "entrance"; there is no "ultimate" position. Only taking your mind, and perfecting its virtues – this is the essence of strategy.

EMPTINESS

The Way of Strategy of the *Ni Tō Ichi Ryū* [Two Swords
One Style] I write out in the scroll of "Emptiness".

The meaning of "Emptiness": where there is not any
objective form, and when things cannot be known,
this is understood as Emptiness.[1]

Of course, "Emptiness" does not exist. Understanding
what is there, you understand what is not there –
this, namely, is Emptiness.

Out in the world, if you view this wrongly, you look
at whatever you cannot understand about things as
"emptiness", but this is not true Emptiness.
All such thinking is misguided.

Also, in this Way of Strategy, as a warrior carrying it out,
the things in a warrior's practice that you do not
understand are not Emptiness. With so many ways to
become lost, people call it "emptiness" when it seems

there is nothing that can be done, but neither is
this true Emptiness.

As members of the warrior class, you should learn the Way
of Strategy correctly, and in addition to this train well in the
other martial arts[2] – the Way that warriors practise never
becoming even a little darkened, your heart never becoming
lost, never neglecting your training for a single morning or
any other time, polishing the twofold heart of [unmoving]
spirit and [active] will,[3] honing the dual eye[4] of perception
and seeing – without the slightest cloud [in your vision]:
you must understand that when the clouds of delusion
clear, *that* is true Emptiness.

As long as you do not yet know the true Way, [it does
not matter] whether [it is] the Buddhist Law or the laws of
the world of men – you will think of them as correct ways,
and believe them to be good things; however, from the
perspective of the true Way,[5] the major "models" and
standards in the world, seen together, are all the biases
of individual minds and, based on these distortions,
go against the true Way.

Understanding this idea, take a place of perfect straightness
as your basis, make the True Mind[6] your Way [of life],
and practise strategy broadly.

Correctly and clearly, taking the large ideas into
your thinking – make Emptiness your Way, and you
will see the Way as Emptiness.

In Emptiness there is Good;
There is no Evil.
There is Wisdom,
There is Principle,
There is the Way –
The Heart
is Emptiness.[7]

Shōhō [Era] Second Year, Fifth Month, Twelfth Day
Shinmen Musashi
[to] Terao Magonojō [honorific]

PART II

HYŌHŌ SANJŪ-GO KA JŌ

"Thirty-five Articles on Strategy"

Having for many years trained in the *Heihō Ni Tō no Ichi Ryū* [Two-Sword Style of Strategy] I now put brush to paper about these things for the first time and humbly submit it. Given your lordship's eminence my words are insufficient and it is difficult to deliver up to you that which I wish to say, but these are the things which we standardly practise, and having grasped the use of the sword in strategy, I am humbly writing out the general ideas of what I have learned.[1]

On naming this Way "Two Swords"

This Way being *Ni Tō* ["Two Swords"], it is the practice to hold two swords (*futatsu no tachi*); there is no holding on with the left hand [as well as the right]. This is to get used to taking up the sword in one hand. Holding the sword in one hand is advantageous in battle formations, on horseback, in rivers and streams, in narrow streets, when taking prisoners; likewise when one has to hold [some other] weapon, or when otherwise in some difficult position, one must [sometimes] take the sword in one hand. When one takes up the sword, at first it feels heavy, but later one becomes able to use it freely. For example, when one learns to shoot a bow, one gains "strength" in that, and when one acquires the ability to ride a horse, there is that

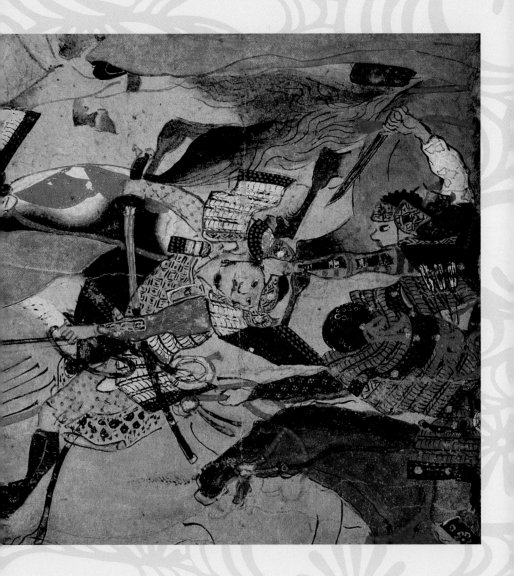

"strength". In the everyday skill of piloting a boat, one takes up the rudder or oars, and there is that "strength". The farmer takes up his shovel and hoe, and becomes powerful in their use. With the sword, too, if one takes it up and learns it, "strength" is something that will develop. That said, people should carry swords appropriate to their bodies, according to their [physical] strength or weakness.

o   o   o

On how to view the Way of Strategy

In this Way, large-scale strategy and individual strategy are similar and both should be thought of in the same way. For example, in what is written here about individual strategy the mind may be thought of as the *taishō*, the hands and feet[2] his ministers and such, and the torso as footsoldiers and farmers; the governance of a country and the training of the body, the large and the small, are in the Way of Strategy both the same. In the training of strategy, the whole body should be thought of entirely as one, leaving nothing out; neither forcefully nor weakly distributing the spirit (*kokoro*) evenly from the top of the head to the bottoms of the feet, and without leaning to any one side, carry out the training.

o   o   o

On how to grasp the sword

When taking up the sword, hold it by "floating" the thumb and index finger, with the middle finger moderately tight, and the ring and little fingers tightly closing. In the sword and in the hand, there is "life" and "death"; when taking a [guard] position, when parrying or when stopping [the opponent's sword] and such, the hand that forgets cutting and becomes fixed is called a "dead hand". What is called "live" is when at any time both the sword and the hand can move easily, without becoming stiff, and cutting well becomes easy: this is called a "living hand". Without curling the wrists, not extending the elbows too much or bending them too much, hold the sword with the sinews on the tops of the forearms relaxed and those on the underside strong. This should be investigated thoroughly.

○ ○ ○

On holding the body

In deportment the face should not be tilted down, nor should it look upwards too much. The shoulders should not be raised or twisted, nor should the chest be thrust out; push the belly forwards, and do not bend at the waist. Do not lock the knees, but make the body straight, showing its width as broad. The idea is to make a point of keeping the body [as it is] for strategy during ordinary life, and in strategy your body will feel (natural and just as) usual. This must be tested exhaustively.

○ ○ ○

On stepping

The use of the feet depends on the occasion; while there are large and small, fast and slow [steps], it is always just like walking normally. Among the [types of] footwork to avoid are "flying" feet, "floating" feet, "creeping" feet, "withdrawing" feet and "back-and-forth" feet – these are all undesirable [types of] footwork. No matter how difficult the place of the footing, you should nonetheless step with certainty. Based on what is written further on, this should be understood in depth.

○   ○   ○

On the setting of the gaze

On the topic of what is called "attaching the eyes" (*me no tsuke*), while long ago there were many ideas, what is called *metsuke* now usually refers to looking at the face. As for how to hold the eyes, look softly while narrowing them slightly more than normal. The eyeballs unmoving, even when the enemy approaches – no matter how close, the eyes are those of looking far away. Seeing with these eyes, one is not taken in by the opponent's techniques, and one can see to both sides as well.

In the two types of seeing, perceiving and looking, the "perceiving eye" should be strong and the "looking eye" weak. There are also eyes that can be said to convey your intentions to the adversary. The will is to be shown in the eyes; the mind is not to be shown. This requires careful investigation.

○   ○   ○

On the assessment of intervals

As for assessing intervals: while there are various other things, in strategy, with regard to the existence of a mind that settles in one place, I will say now that there should be no such mind.

No matter what the Way [being pursued], if one becomes accustomed to this thing,[3] it can be understood well.

In general, when your sword is close enough to a person to hit them, that person's sword, too, is close enough to hit you.

If you intend to strike a person, you must forget your own body. You must work this out rigorously.

o   o   o

On mindset

Regarding the setting of the mind: without weakening, becoming entangled, trying to figure things out, or fearing, make the heart full of intent and the mind broad and like water. According to the situation, the mind is one that adapts to things. Water has a deep blue colour. There are single drops. There are vast oceans. This should be investigated deeply.

o   o   o

On understanding high, middle and low levels of strategy

In strategy there are bodily positions. Also in the sword there are various positions and the [styles of] strategy that show them, making them appear slow or showing them as fast – these should be understood as the low level. Then there are [styles of] strategy that show off techniques as being very complicated, or present them as being especially rhythmical; those wares being popular, they try to make them look impressive. These [styles of] strategy are of the middle level. Strategy of the upper level is neither

forceful nor weak, is not showy, nor fast; it does not appear impressive, but neither does it present itself badly. Strategy that is made broad and straight, and which appears calm and quiet – this is the highest level. This should be investigated well.

o   o   o

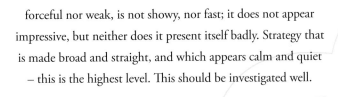

On the "measuring cord"

Always keep a measuring cord in mind. For all opponents, if you hold a measuring cord up to them, [you will see their] strong places, weak places, straight places, warped places, places where they tense and places where they slacken. Make your mind become a measure, and apply it quickly, pulling the cord and observing; [in this way] a person's mind can be understood well. According to that measure, the round and the angled, the long and the short, the twisted and the straight, all should be understood well. This should be worked on.

o   o   o

On the path of the sword

If the path of the sword is not understood well, it is difficult to swing the sword without disturbing the mind.[4] Moreover, do not be forceful, misunderstanding use of the ridge or flat of the blade, or try to use the sword like a small knife. Likewise, if handled in the manner of something like a rice-scoop, in the crucial moment of cutting down the enemy, it is difficult to use. Always discerning the path of the sword, wield the sword calmly, as if with a very heavy blade, and train in such a way as to cut the enemy well.

o   o   o

On "striking" and "hitting"

As regards "striking" and "hitting", both of them are involved in the use of the sword. Learning clearly how to strike, as by cutting test targets and such, you become able to strike as you intend. Then, as for "hitting", when you cannot see a decisive strike, it is possible to just hit anywhere. Even if you hit, and even if very hard, it is not the same as striking. Whether you hit the enemy's body or hit [his] sword, hit or miss you do not really trouble him; if you do not truly strike, your arms and legs can give away your movements. This needs to be worked out diligently.

o   o   o

On the "three initiatives"

As for the three initiatives, one is the initiative when you attack the enemy. Second is the initiative when the enemy attacks you. The third is the initiative when both you and the enemy attack [at the same time]. These are the three initiatives. In the initiative when you attack first, make your body an attacking body, keep mind and legs[5] centred, and without slackening or tensing, disrupt the enemy's mind.[6] This is the initiative of attack. Then there is when the enemy comes to attack; remove all intention from your body, and when he comes quite close, you should free your mind, and following from the enemy's movement immediately take the intitiative yourself. Finally, when you attack each other at the same time, make your whole body strong and relaxed: in the sword, in the body, in the legs and in the mind. In this way you should take the initiative. To seize the initiative is crucial.

o o o

On "crossing a ford"

When both the enemy and you are close enough to hit one another, and you strike with your sword, but you think the enemy will get inside your strike, you should close in tightly to the right with both your body and legs. Getting across the ford, [7] you have nothing to worry about. To understand this, you must analyze carefully what I have written previously about initiative.

o o o

On the body that replaces the sword

What is called "the body that replaces the sword" is that when the sword strikes out, the body does not waver. Or the idea that when appearing to strike the body, the sword strikes [as if] from the target itself. This is the empty mind. There is no case where the sword, body and mind all strike at the same time. The centred mind, the centred body – these must be diligently studied.

o o o

On "two feet"

By "two feet", what is meant is that during one strike with the sword, both feet are moved. When the sword presses down or releases, when you advance or retreat, there are "two feet" – the feeling of this is that the feet are connected. If with one sword strike only one foot is moved, this leads to fixity. If thought of as a pair, the feet are just as they are when walking normally. This should be worked out comprehensively.

o   o   o

On "stomping down the sword"

This is the idea of treading down the tip of the [enemy's] sword with your foot. At the point where the strike of an enemy's attacking sword falls, it can be trodden on with your left foot. When stomping, do it with your sword, with your body and with your spirit. If you attack with the initiative, you will be in a position to win, no matter what. If you do not have this mindset, you will wind up just hitting back and forth, and this is a very bad thing. There are times when the feet rest, though; stomping down the sword is not something that can be done all the time. This must be investigated carefully.

o   o   o

On "stifling the shadow"
(Kage wo osayuru) [8]

"Stifling the shadow" means if you see into the enemy's body, there are places where his mind is overly occupied, and places where it is insufficiently engaged. If you draw his attention where his mind is already overly concentrated, and suddenly thrust your sword in the shadow where it is lacking, the enemy's rhythym will be disrupted, and it will be easy to win. However, it is essential for your mind to remain fully engaged and not to miss the place to strike. This requires refinement.

o o o

On "moving the form" (Kage wo ugokasu)

This *kage* is the positive form (*yō no kage*). Forestall the enemy's attack, and when he comes out and takes up a position, the idea is to suppress the enemy's sword, making your body empty. If you strike with your sword at the place where the enemy emerges, the enemy's body will definitely move. If he moves, it is easy to win. We did not use to train like this. Now, you should avoid allowing the mind to become fixed anywhere, and strike where [the enemy] comes out. This requires extensive investigation.

o o o

On "loosening the bowstring"

With regard to "loosening the bowstring": there are occasions when both your enemy's mind and yours are pulled taut. It is important to quickly loosen the body, the sword, the legs and the mind. When your enemy least expects it, detach completely. This needs to be worked on.

o o o

On the teaching of "the small comb"

The idea of the small comb means to untangle knots. Keeping in your mind a small comb, when your enemy tries to tie you

up, depending on whatever he does, the idea is to disentangle [yourself]. "Tying up" and "pulling taut" are similar, but "pulling taut" has a very strong spirit, and "tying up" has a weak spirit. This should be studied extensively.

o   o   o

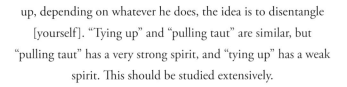

On understanding the intervals in rhythms

As for understanding the intervals in rhythms, according to the particular adversary, some are fast, and some are slow; the rhythm depends on the opponent. With an opponent whose spirit is slow, when it comes to crossing swords, do not move your body, and without letting on what your sword will do, quickly strike out of nowhere. This is "one beat". For an enemy whose spirit is fast, you should strike with both body and spirit, and then after the enemy moves, strike him there. This is what is called "two advances". Then there is what is called "no thought, no form": without your body giving any appearance of the intent to strike, leaving your mind and swords as they are, in coordination with the enemy's energy, strike powerfully out of nowhere. This is "no thought, no form". Furthermore, as pertains to "delayed rhythm", when the opponent tries to slap away your sword or parry it, becoming extremely slow, with the feeling of stagnating in the middle, and striking in the interval – this is "delayed rhythm". Thorough practice is necessary.

o   o   o

On "holding the pillow down"

"Holding the pillow down" means when you get a feeling that the enemy is about to strike with his sword, from out of nowhere you quash that intention to strike at its beginning. In quashing it, quash it with your spirit, quash it with your body and quash it with your swords. If you understand this feeling, it is good for striking the enemy, for getting in on him [into his space], for getting away, and for taking the initiative. It is an idea that can be used in any situation. It is vital to train in this.

o o o

On "understanding the situation"

By "understanding the situation" what is meant is that it is necessary to see and understand well the conditions of that place, and the situation of the enemy: the conditions of rising or sinking, shallowness or depth, strength or weakness. By the constant practise of the "measuring cord", the situation can be assessed immediately, on the spot. Seeing and taking in the situation of the moment, you win whether facing forwards or facing back. This should be considered deeply.

o o o

On "becoming the adversary"

You should think of your own body as the adversary's. Whether you are dealing with someone who has retreated into an easily defended place, or a very large opponent,[9] or when you

encounter someone who is very accomplished in that Way,[10] you should think of the sense of difficulty in his mind. If the adversary's mind is misled, without realizing it, he will think of a weak person as strong, imagine a person unskilled in the Way as one who is very accomplished, and see a small opponent as a large one. It is possible for an enemy to take a thing without advantage for an advantage. "Becoming the adversary", you should analyse this extensively.

o   o   o

On retaining/releasing the mind [11]

Retaining the mind or releasing the mind is something that depends on the situation and the time. When you take up swords, usually the mind of will (*i no kokoro*) is released and that of spirit (*shin no kokoro*) is retained. On the other hand, when you strike an enemy decisively, the spirit is let loose and the will is held onto. There are a variety of ways to view retaining the mind or releasing the mind. This should be investigated deeply.

o   o   o

On the "opportune hit" [12]

What is called the "opportune hit" is when the enemy comes in close to cut with his sword, and with your sword you either slap his sword aside, or parry it, or just hit him; whether slapping, parrying or hitting, the opponent's sword [attack] should be thought of as an opportunity. Whether "riding" [the enemy's

sword], slipping it or sticking to it, if these are all for the purpose of striking, your body, mind and sword all will always have the intention of striking. You need to study this carefully.

○ ○ ○

On the "stickiness of lacquer-glue"

The "stickiness of lacquer-glue" means getting right up next to your opponent. From legs to hips to head, without any opening, stick completely, as sticking objects together with lacquer-glue. If there is a place where you do not stick to his body, the enemy can employ various techniques. The rhythm of sticking to the opponent should be one of a calm spirit, like that of "holding the pillow down".

○ ○ ○

On the "body of the autumn monkey"

The "body of the autumn monkey": when sticking to the adversary, you should stick to his body, with the feeling of having no hands.[13] What is bad is leaving the body back and extending the hands. If the hands are extended, the body tends to retreat. Although from the left[14] shoulder to the forearm is useful, the extended hands are not. The rhythm of sticking to the opponent is the same as before.

○ ○ ○

On "comparing heights"

What is called "comparing heights" is how, when you get right up next to the enemy, as if comparing heights with him, you extend your body, with the feeling of showing that you are the taller. The rhythm of getting up close is the same idea as with anything else. This should be investigated carefully.

o o o

On the teaching of "the door" [15]

What is called the "hinge body" is when going to stick to the opponent, you first make the breadth of your body wide and straight, as though trying to hide both the opponent's sword and body behind it. Stick in such a way that there is no opening between the enemy's body and yours. Then when coming alongside him, turn sideways, presenting yourself as extremely narrow and straight, and slam your shoulder strongly into his chest; this is a body [positioning] for knocking the opponent down. It should be worked on.

o o o

On the teaching of "the general and the troops"

What is meant by "the general and the troops" is that having absorbed the principles of strategy into your body, you come to see the opponent as the troops, and you yourself become the general, not giving the enemy even the slightest freedom, not allowing him either to swing his sword or thrust with it.

Realizing that everything submits to your intent, you should make it so that the opponent cannot even conceive a tactic in his mind. This is an essential thing.

○   ○   ○

On "position, no-position"

As regards "position, no-position": this is what happens in the body when you take up swords. No matter what, the body is in a position, but if you have the intention to "take a position", both the sword and the body become fixed. Act according to the place and the situation; while you always have swords, there is no thought of the taking of a position in your mind. For your sword to be appropriate to the enemy, within the raised attitude there are three types,[16] and within the the middle and lowered attitudes[17] there are also three different ideas (*mittsu no kokoro*). It is the same thing for the left and right sides. Even if you are standing firm, the idea is that there is "no-position". This should be investigated dilligently.

○   ○   ○

On the "body of a massive rock"

The "body of a massive rock" means getting rid of movement, and making your spirit (*kokoro*) strong and large. If for yourself you acquire with your body the many principles,[18] [training] unceasingly, any living thing will want to get out of your way. Even the insentient grasses and trees will have trouble taking root, and the falling rain and the blowing wind will have the same feeling. This body should be studied well.

○ ○ ○

On understanding the moment

With regard to what is called "understanding the moment": understand fast moments, and slow ones; understand the moments when you can get away, and understand those when escape is impossible. In this style there is a deep essence known as "direct transmission". These things are passed down orally.

○ ○ ○

On "myriad Principles, a single Emptiness" (Banri-ikku) [19]

I humbly submit that the point of myriad Principles but a single Emptiness is impossible to write about, and so it would be best if you could kindly meditate on this for yourself.[20] In the preceeding thirty-five articles[21] I have humbly attempted to write out a general outline of the mindset for strategy and how it should be viewed. If in a few places I have neglected to offer up some points, they would all be similar to what is here above. In addition, this style is practised and acquired individually, so the specifics of the movement of the sword, and other such things which are conveyed orally, do not need to be written here. Furthermore, should there be any places about which your lordship has any doubt, it would be best if you would allow me humbly to explain them to you myself.

○ ○ ○

Kan'ei [Era] Eighteenth Year, Second Month, an Auspicious Day[22]
Shinmen Musashi Genshin

PART III

DOKKŌDŌ

"The Path Walked Alone"[1]

Do not ignore the many ways in the world.

Do not seek after pleasures for yourself.

Do not rely on anything whatsoever.

Think little about yourself; think deeply about the world.

Never, in all your life, think greedy or desirous thoughts.

Hold no regrets about your personal affairs.

No matter what, never be jealous of others.

On whatever the path, do not be sad about parting ways.

Do not complain about or blame either yourself or others.

Do not allow your thinking to be led down the paths
of romantic feelings.

Cultivate no likings for particular things.

Have no special wishes about your home.

Do not have a preference for delicacies.

Do not hold on to old equipment in order to pass it
down to posterity.

Regarding your body, do not avoid certain things
for superstitious reasons.[2]

Do not concern yourself with an unnecessary variety
of tools, especially weapons.

Along the way, have no bad feelings toward death.

Do not seek to be rich in your old age.

Buddha and the gods are to be revered, but do not make
requests of them.

Even if you must surrender your life, never abandon
your honour.

Always stay on the path of strategy, and never stray from it.

Shōho [Era] Second Year, Fifth Month, Second Day
Shinmen Musashi

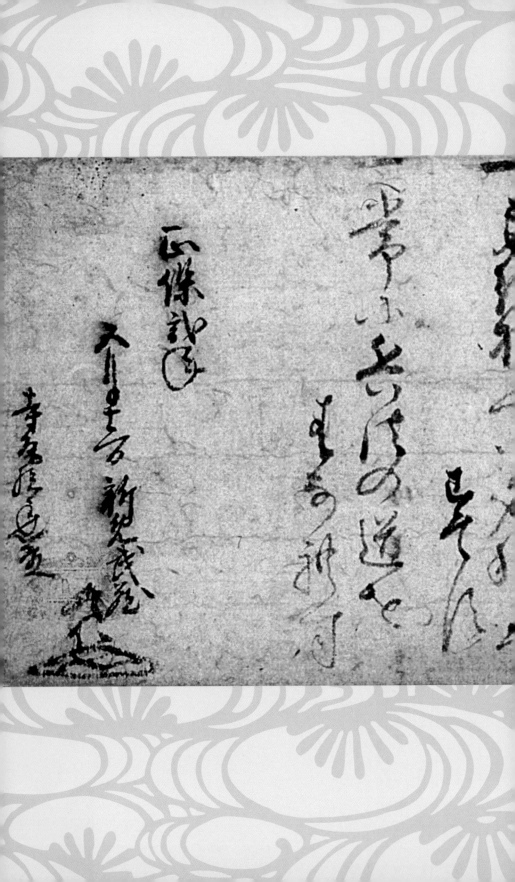

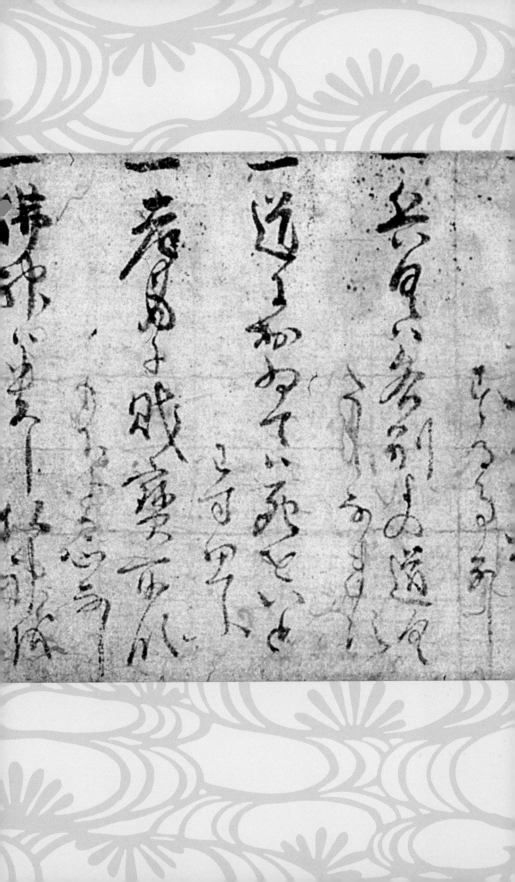

ENDNOTES
Introduction

[1] These texts were the bases for two others, the *Bukōden* serving as the basis for the *Nitenki*, and the *Bushū Denraiki* for the *Heihō Senshi Denki*. However, this second generation of accounts was written more than a hundred years after Musashi's death, and though they sought to improve what their writers saw as the insufficiencies of the earlier works, most scholars agree that the earlier works are the more reliable.

[2] "Shinmen" (新免) or "newly absolved" referred to a branch of the powerful Fujiwara clan, which had been exiled for its part in an attempt to restore Emperor Godaigo, but was later forgiven – hence the name. The Hirata were the branch's vassals and Munisai married a woman from the Shinmen; he and his son Musashi were allowed to take the name by extension. "Musashi no Kami" would have indicated nominal jurisdiction over an area called Musashi (武蔵: "warriors' storehouse"), of which there have been, like "Miyamoto", any number of places bearing the name. With "Fujiwara no Genshin" Musashi stakes his claim to ancestry of one of Japan's oldest noble houses, the aforementioned Fujiwara. Genshin was his Buddhist name.

[3] Miyamoto-Sanomo was then in Mimasaka province. Two other towns, Miyamoto-mura (which in fact was in Harima), and Yoneda-mura (also in Harima), also lay claim to being Musashi's birthplace, but records seem to point to Sanomo as being the most likely.

[4] The *jitte* or *jutte* (十手), meaning "ten hand", referred to an iron bar with a handle and a prong on one or both sides, or a rake-like object; both were defensive weapons, used primarily for disarming opponents wielding swords.

[5] A *dōjō* (道場) is literally a "Way-place", a special area set aside for the practice of a particular tradition (usually with a spiritual aspect) known as a Way (*dō* 道). The word is most closely associated with schools of the martial arts, but other traditions such as *zazen* meditation and *shodō* calligraphy are practised in halls or studios known as *dōjō*.

[6] 円明流: This could be interpreted as "Circle of Brightness Style", or alternatively "Perfect Clarity Style". The word for circle is often used to stand for perfection or completeness, and the word "bright" can also mean "clear". It has additionally been speculated that the name referred to Musashi holding his two swords with the tips close together or touching, forming a sort of circle, although there is no clear evidence that this was the case.

[7] The Myōshinji tradition, somewhat unusually, allowed for "custom" *kōan* to be created for students, rather than using the standard canon (such as "What is the sound of one hand clapping?"). This approach probably would have suited the fiercely iconoclastic Musashi very well, possibly better than other more traditional schools.

[8] The *mizukuruma* is a circular "windmilling" technique in which the swordsman moves forward, cutting up from below in large arcs; the *tsubame-gaeshi* mimics the sudden turn of a swallow in flight, especially out of a dive.

[9] Unlike the usual billowing *hakama* 袴, whose wide openings at the ends of the legs flapped around the wearer's ankles like a loose skirt, the *karusan* were loose in the hips and thighs but snug around the shins, making them ideal for workers and warriors (the name comes from the Portuguese *calçaō*, as they were originally seen on Portuguese sailors).

[10] There is some discrepancy as to whether this Lord Matsudaira was Matsudaira Naomasa or Katsutaka, and whether it occurred at Matsue or Matsuyama Castle. The time is also somewhat in dispute; some place this event after Musashi had moved to Kokura, on a trip to Edo.

[11] 思い者：literally "thought-of person"; sometimes applied to a lover but at the time also a common euphemism for a prostitute.

[12] A clan whose influence as instructors of swordsmanship was far reaching, but whose overall power did not rival the Hosokawa.

[13] According to the *Bukōden* this actually occurred while Musashi was still in residence at Kokura, but when he was on a visit to Kumamoto.

[14] *Renga* is a form of collaborative poetry in which the writers alternate verses, or in larger groups continue them in a circle. The set of rules involves key words or images that must link one verse to the next.

[15] Bodhidharma was a Buddhist monk who is traditionally believed to have brought Buddhism to China, specifically in the Zen tradition (called Ch'an in Chinese; the Sanskrit is Dhyāna). Known as Daruma in Japanese, the often bearded and wild-looking monk was a popular subject for *suibokuga* ink paintings. Another Chinese tradition names Bodhidharma/Daruma as the original founder of the Shaolin Temple style of martial arts (though this seems highly unlikely). A prominent figure in Japanese culture, he figures in children's games, and a ball-like image of his head without the eyes painted in is used as a good-luck charm: when a wish is made or a goal decided, one eye is painted in, and then when the wish is granted or the objective achieved the other is painted in, and the image is dedicated at a temple (traditionally, the larger the wish or the objective, the larger the head).

16 Although the actual governing power rested squarely with the *bakufu* military dictatorship, the emperors in Kyōto continued to be enthroned, but only as figureheads, with no actual power. It is from the changing emperors that the Japanese eras get their names and numbering, starting again with each new emperor, a tradition that continues to this day (at the time of writing, year twenty-three of the Heisei reign: 2011 in Western year numbering).

17 Shingon (真言 "True Word") Buddhism is an esoteric sect of Buddhism, the fundamental tenet of which is that Sanskrit, the language of the Budhha, itself is sacred and holds the key to enlightenment. Brought to Japan from China in the early ninth century by the monk Kūkai, Shingon is focused almost entirely on rituals. Members of the Shingon sect recite *mantra*s in Sanskrit and perform a variety of *mudra*s (esoteric hand positions), which are believed to call upon the guidance and assistance of various deities. High significance is attached to the characters of Sanskrit writing as well.

18 Though not, perhaps, particularly ardent an adherent, given his exhortation in the *Dokkōdō* that "Buddha and the gods are to be revered, but [one should] not make requests of them."

19 Zen was most closely linked with warriors, going back to the Kamakura period. The Zen emphasis on self-reliance and austere aesthetics appealed to the warrior class, and its focus on the practice of clearing the mind completely (rather than on prayers, *mantra*s, and so on) allowed warriors to heighten their awareness and sharpen their battle skills. Shingon was less widely practised by the warrior class (but famously by the *ninja* clans). The secretive nature of esoteric Buddhism seems a natural match for the *ninja*, but it is a little hard to say what about it would have appealed to warriors like the Yagyū and Musashi.

20 According to the *Bukōden* there were thirty-nine articles at this time.

21 Tsukahara Bokuden (1489–1571) was another swordsman later venerated as a *kensei*, said to have fought and won as many as 200 bouts. After learning the *Katori Shintō Ryū* Bokuden developed his own style, which he called the *Kashima Shintō Ryū*, at the Kashima Shrine, in what is now Ibaraki prefecture. These two styles are both mentioned specifically by Musashi in "Ground", and not in a particularly generous light. Interestingly, a popular story has a young Musashi meeting Bokuden as a very old man, not knowing who he is, and when they eventually come to blows Bokuden deflects all of Musashi's attacks with a pot lid. The story is pure fiction, however, as Tsukahara died well before Musashi was even born.

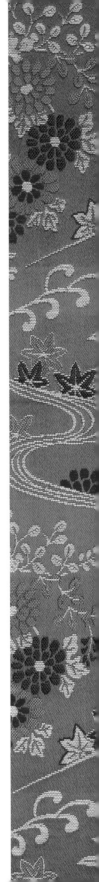

Go Rin no Sho
Ground

[1] 二 "Two" 天 "Heaven" 一 "One" 流 "Flow" – this last character, *ryū*, is a word used to designate styles or schools of technique in the various arts. However, the words "style" and "school" have a sense of codification, of solidity, and do not properly convey the idea of the techniques "flowing" from teacher to student. Musashi uses this name for his style only twice; otherwise, he uses the term "Two Sword Style" or "Two Swords One Style" ("One Flow") variously. In his younger years, Musashi called his style the *Enmei Ryū* (円明流), or "Bright Circle Style". Presumably Musashi changed the name after his enlightenment to the Way; "Two Heavens" (二天 *Ni Ten*) was also the pen-name he used to sign and seal his calligraphy later in life.

[2] 1643

[3] What is now the Kumamoto area.

[4] A *bodhisattva* is one who has achieved enlightenment but delays becoming a true *buddha* until all others have also been saved. Kannon (観音) is the goddess of mercy, derived from the Chinese Guanyin.

[5] Present-day Hyōgo prefecture.

[6] Or "Single flow".

[7] The traditional Japanese calendar system and way of counting hours was based on the Chinese zodiac; the day was divided into twelve two-hour units analogous to the twelve-year zodiac cycle. The hour of the tiger was the two hours just before sunrise, roughly 3am to 5am.

[8] Japanese society at the time included an "untouchable" class known as *eta/weta* or *hinin* (非人), responsible for such "unclean" jobs as the disposal of the dead, the tanning of leather, and working in prisons. Discrimination against people from such bloodlines, later known as *burakumin*, continued well into the modern era and has not yet disappeared completely.

[9] Hitachi was mostly in the present-day prefecture of Ibaraki. Musashi writes the names of the shrines out phonetically; today the "Kantori" shrine is known as Katori.

[10] "Ten Abilities and Seven Arts" was a term used to refer to the various skills learned in the education of the samurai clans – such as swordsmanship, calligraphy and oration – and their applications. The numbers became a matter of tradition, but the actual content was not clearly defined, and seem to have varied in interpretation.

11 *Bonjin* (凡人); that is, not nobles or members of the clergy.

12 *Shi-nō-kō-shō* (士農工商): more literally "gentry, farmer, artisan, merchant" – this is a four-character Chinese compound from Confucian teachings, expressing society's four elements, each of which has obligations to and connections with the others. I have rearranged the order to conform to the sequence in which Musashi presents them.

13 Musashi seems to be referring critically to the tendency of the samurai clans, starting in the early Edo Era (1600s), to focus more on cultural refinements rather than predominantly on the martial arts.

14 Most likely the Four Houses of the Fujiwara, but it could be any number of famous "Four Houses" here, or all of them generically.

15 Here Musashi uses the word *yabure* in phonetic script, which could mean either 破れ "breaking apart" or 敗れ "being defeated"; I have used the former, in keeping with the physical metaphor of the house.

16 The characters in question are 大 (*dai*) "large, great" and 工 (*ku*) "skill, technical ability, technology".

17 Sliding paper lattice-work doors.

18 Here Musashi uses the word *taiyu*, and writes it in phonetic script (たいゆう), which leaves it open to a number of interpretations. It could also be "morale", but this seems redundant with the following sentence.

19 *Kokoro* (心); this could also be rendered as "heart", "mind", or "spirit", but here I believe "mindset" is closest to the intended meaning.

20 "Ten thousand" is a single character in Sino–Japanese script, and in both languages it is used to mean "very many" or "countless".

21 A *shaku* is approximately 30cm, or a little less than a foot.

22 The character for "wind" (風) can also, when used with its Chinese-based reading of *fū*, mean "style".

23 That is, an esoteric or exoteric concept. Musashi here uses the words *oku* (奥), meaning "deep interior", and *kuchi* (口), a mouth or other opening – or in this case, "entrance". Traditionally, schools of the martial arts divided their teachings into *oku* "interior" or *ura* (裏) "reverse/hidden", and *omote* (表) "surface" or "entrance". The former teachings were secret and guarded, the latter made visible to the public and taught to beginners (this practice is continued by some styles today). Musashi claims that in his style there are no such distinctions.

24 The *tachi*, (太刀 or "broad" sword) was originally worn hung from the belt by straps, blade side down; it was made to be easily drawn while in armour and/or on horseback. The *katana*, at that time, was a shorter sword worn thrust in the belt. When the *bushi* became more gentrified, they began to wear both the long and the short sword under the belt, blade up, with their daily attire, as a mark of status. The name *katana* came to be applied to the longer sword, and the shorter one became known as the *wakizashi* (脇差), or "thrust through at the side", probably because this was the one regularly worn all the time, even indoors. *Katana*, now written as a single character (刀), originally derives from two: *kata* (片), meaning "one side" and *na* or *ha* (刃), meaning "blade". *The tachi* originally evolved from the older *chokutō* (直刀), which was straight and double-edged, like most medieval western straight blades. So the term *katana*, for a curved, single-edged weapon, probably originally served to distinguish it from a straighter, double-edged one. Musashi mixes the conventional sets of terms, almost always referring to the long sword as the *tachi*, and the shorter as the *wakizashi*; after his brief history of the nomenclature, he does not use the word *katana* again.

²⁵ This is the name Musashi generally uses, only referring to the style as *Ni Ten Ichi Ryū* occasionally. See also note 1 earlier.

²⁶ The *naginata* is basically a long pole with a short sword blade attached to the end; in fact, the characters used for the word today (長刀) mean simply "long/extended sword". It resembles what in Europe was known as a glaive, but with a narrower blade than most glaives. The *naginata* also lacks a hook, meant for pulling a rider off his horse, which is usually a feature of the glaive.

²⁷ Here Musashi uses the old terms *tachi* for the long sword and *katana* for the short; since he uses the other terms a few lines later they are translated here to avoid confusion.

²⁸ Some schools of swordsmanship in Musashi's time mandated a certain length for the swords they used, some of which were particularly long or short.

²⁹ Somewhat oddly given the heading, Musashi does not actually discuss the literal meaning of these characters here (perhaps he considered it too self-evident, a strong possibility in a language where the literal meaning of words is generally inherent in their ideograms). The two characters Musashi refers to are 兵法, which can be read either *hei-hō* or *hyō-hō*. The first character means "soldier" and the second "law", "rule" or "method"; in Chinese the compound already had come to mean "strategy" – predominantly military strategy, but also extended to include strategy in general. Musashi specifically explains later that his interpretation of "strategy", although mainly intended to be applied militarily, is not limited to this definition. As Musashi notes as well, the word also was (and still is) often applied to mean any of the specific martial arts such as *kenjutsu* (swordsmanship) or *jūjutsu*, or all of them generically. Again, Musashi explicitly states that this is not what he means when using the term.

[30] The word Musashi uses here is *bugei* (武芸), which is quite literally "war art[s]", and which is distinct from "strategy".

[31] That is, in a *dōjō*.

[32] One *ken* is six *shaku* (see note 21), or approximately 6ft (1.82m). Thus the distance Musashi describes is about 118ft (36m).

[33] Literally, "at right", as the scroll reads from right to left.

[34] 1645

[35] Terao Magonojō Nobumasa (1611–1672), one of Musashi's favourite students. With his brother Terao Motomenosuke Nobuyuki (1621–1688), he was one of three men chosen to carry on the *Ni Ten Ichi Ryū*.

[36] 1667

[37] This later inscription is in a markedly different hand from the rest of the text in the extant copy. The *Bukōden* indicates that Terao Magonojō passed on his copy of the *Go Rin no Sho* to Yamamoto Gennosuke after making him heir to his branch of the *Ni Ten Ichi Ryū* schoo. "Terao Yumeyo Katsunobu" may have been an alternate name used by Magonojō later in his life. This was not unusual at the time – Musashi was known by a different name in his youth.

Water

[1] Tellingly, Musashi here uses a Buddhist term, *setsuna* (刹那): in the time it takes to snap one's fingers, there are sixty or sixty-five *setsuna*. This term was used to denote an infinitesimally small amount of time.

[2] I have translated the word *kokoro* (心) as both "spirit" and "mind".

[3] The word here is literally "eyeballs" (*me no tama* 目の玉), but I believe the sense is conveyed.

[4] That is, in actual battle.

[5] Test-cutting was practised on wetted rolls of old straw *tatami* mats, human corpses, or sometimes even on live prisoners who had been condemned to death. (See also note 5 in "Wind".)

[6] It should be noted that the Japanese word used here – *ashi* (足) – includes both the foot and the leg. (The word for "hand" – *te* 手 – can likewise include both the hand and the arm.)

[7] Generally speaking, a "raised" position is one where the sword is held above shoulder-level, a "middle" position is one in which the sword is held between shoulder- and waist-level, and a "lowered" position is one with the sword held below waist level.

[8] Earlier Musashi only uses the word 道 (*michi* or *dō*), which has numerous possible interpretations, but here he uses the word *michi-suji* (道筋), which

has a specifically physical meaning of "route", "path" or "passage", and thus it is clear that throughout this section he is discussing the physical path of the sword rather than any more philosophical "Way".

⁹ Musashi here is most likely referring to the *tessen* (鉄扇), an iron fan used as a military signal but also as a weapon, rather than an ordinary fan.

¹⁰ The word here is 小刀 *kogatana*, or "little sword", meaning a small knife like a pocketknife. These two characters can also be read *shōtō* and mean "short sword", but this is a historically later reading. Musashi would refer to the short sword as the *wakizashi*, or perhaps the *kodachi* ("small *tachi*"), and here clearly means the small knife.

¹¹ The term used here is *omote* (usually 表, but here written phonetically), which means "outer" or "surface". Techniques in Japanese martial arts are commonly divided into *omote*, which is the standard or basic form, and *ura* (裏, "behind"), which are all the possible variants of that basic form depending on actual conditions.

¹² This term, *kissaki-gaeshi* (切っ先返し), or "cutting-point return", is somewhat difficult to explain, but involves quickly flipping the blade of the sword around to cut in the opposite direction.

¹³ *Kosu hyōshi* (こす拍子) "crossing-over rhythm"– because *kosu* here is written in *hiragana* phonetic script, there is some dispute as to the interpretation of this expression. The most common interpretation is that *kosu* is (越す) "to cross/pass over" – as in a mountain pass – and this interpretation has a certain logic. However, although the *kanji* is the same, I believe here it is most closely related to *sen wo kosu* (先を越す), literally "pass/cross over the point" but meaning "to forestall". The first documented use of this latter expression dates to 1656, more than ten years after Musashi's death, but it seems probable that this sense of the word was already in use, and this meaning makes much more sense than others in this context.

¹⁴ There is no real way to tell which Way Musashi means here, but because he is dealing specifically with swordsmanship in this passage I am inclined to read this as meaning the Way of Swordsmanship, or possibly the Way of the Warrior in general. However, it is possible that he means, even more generally, the Way of Strategy.

¹⁵ This is the same word (*ukete* 受て, a form of *ukeru*, "to receive") that I have translated earlier as "parry", but which also can have the sense of "understand" or "grasp" [comprehend]. I believe the latter is intended here, although it is possible a double meaning is being employed.

¹⁶ *Ni no koshi* (二のこし). *Koshi* here appears in phonetic *hiragana* script, and has been interpreted by some as 腰 (*koshi*), a word for the hips and

lower abdomen/back as a unit; however, I believe the word intended here is
越し (also *koshi*), meaning "to pass" or "to advance over". It also occurs in the
expression *sen wo kosu* (先を越す), which means to forestall someone's attack.
The latter interpretation is much more intelligible in the context; another
translation might be "double-forestalling".

[17] *Mu-nen mu-sō* 無念無相 – this is all Buddhist terminology and extremely
close to a common expression meaning "free from all thought", read in fact
exactly the same way: *mu-nen mu-sō*, but with a different character for *sō*
(想), which means "idea, concept". Thus the other expression is "no thought,
no concept", but in Musashi's text here the character for *sō* is very close to
the former but slightly different – 相, meaning "form" or "aspect", giving
us 無相 "no form, formless", another Buddhist term. Although it has been
suggested this may have been merely a copying error, I believe the use of
the different term to be deliberate, especially since the same character is
used both times, and in virtually all copies of the text.

[18] *Kurai* くらい, written in phonetic *hiragana* script, could also mean "rank"
or "status"; that is, you must assess your opponent's level of skill accurately.

[19] Despite the heading, "strike" is the word used here. Musashi is inconsistent
with this terminology, which is strange, given his very clear distinction
between "striking" and "hitting" elsewhere. "Blow" I have used to translate
the same word as "hit", but it is in-between enough that this could probably
be "blow" too, without any real change in meaning (in English).

[20] Literally "crimson leaves" (*kōyō* 紅葉), which refers to the Japanese maple or
momiji, and how in autumn its leaves fall from the tree at the slightest touch.

[21] "Tagging", as in the children's game, might actually be a more appropriate
image for the meaning here.

[22] *Shūkō* – Musashi writes this out in phonetic *hiragana* (しうこう) in the
heading, and then in *kanji* (秋猿) in the next line. There is a common
misperception that *shūkō*, or "autumn monkey", refers to a monkey with
short arms; in fact, quite the opposite is true. The monkey referred to as the
shūkō in Musashi's day characteristically has extremely *long* arms, as can be
clearly seen in illustrations from the time. Why then would Musashi choose
to represent the idea of *not* extending the arms with the image of a
long-armed monkey? The answer probably lies in a Buddhist fable in which
a monkey (generally depicted as a long-armed specimen) spies the moon
reflected in a stream. He reaches out to try to scoop it up, and falls into the
water. It can be assumed that afterwards such a monkey would no longer
extend its arms so far out. This was a well-known story in Musashi's time,
and the mere mention of a monkey would have hinted at this connotation.

[23] *Teki utsu mae* (敵打前) "adversary strike before" – lacking postparticles,

this is unclear; I have read it as *teki wo utsu mae* ("before striking your
adversary"), but it could also mean "before your adversary strikes". I believe
the former is more logical here, and is in keeping with the explanation in
"The body replaces the sword".

[24] The word used here is 間, which means "interval", and can be read *ma* or
aida; in either case it can indicate either space or time. The former seemed
to make more sense here, but it could refer to the latter, or possibly both.

[25] Anyone who has ever watched two boxers staring each other down at the
centre of the ring before a match can imagine this clearly.

[26] As noted before, one *ken* is about 6ft (1.82m), so it is suggested this
technique can knock an opponent back by 12–18ft (3.6m–5.5m).

[27] That is, the two swords form an X, catching the opponent's sword and
trapping him at the same time.

[28] This section seems to be in error somehow, because the reference to the left
hand punching would apparently apply only to the third type of parry. I see
two possibilities: one is that the introductory phrase should actually be "in
this third parry"; the other is that the inclusion of "left" was in error, and this
should simply say "clenching your hand into a fist".

[29] This is, on the one hand, a sort of visualization technique, but not only
that, in the sense that the objective is not necessarily to actually stab the
opponent in the face. However, if you keep that in mind, the opponent will
perceive it and react to it (perhaps even if only subconsciously), which
creates openings for you.

[30] These terms come from Zen Buddhism and are basically meaningless
shouts meant to startle an adept out of conscious thought and into
enlightenment. The written phonetic *tsu* in Japanese sometimes represents
a stop or hitch in pronunciation; in practice this generally sounds like
"*kah-toh!*" with each sound somewhat clipped.

[31] Literally, "even before you slap", or "faster than you slap".

[32] Interestingly, here Musashi uses the word *tachi* for both swords, even
though just previous he refers to them as the *katana* and *wakizashi*. Thus it
can be seen that Musashi uses the word *tachi* very generically for "sword",
and in any place where he does so may be referring to either the long or the
short sword, or both.

[33] The word used here, *uozunagi* ("fish linked-up"), could also possibly refer
to a number of fish hooked on a line, but that did not seem consistent with
the idea of "chasing them around".

[34] Here by itself is the phrase *kuden* (口伝), which means "oral transmission",
usually by which a traditional art is passed down. This phrase is oddly abrupt
in the text, and it seems likely that it may have been a margin note by one of

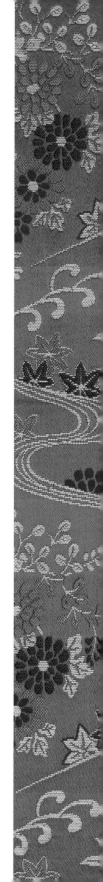

Musashi's disciples, perhaps Terao Magonojō, and mistakenly transcribed into a later version.

[35] This seems to be more of a spiritual concept than an actual "technique" – an idea of so totally dominating the opponent with your spirit that you cut them down at once with a single blow, without them ever having a chance. Many schools of swordsmanship, including the *Ittō*, *Shin-Kage* and *Musō Shindō* styles, feature some teaching of this kind.

[36] See note 34.

[37] Way of Swordsmanship, since Musashi is clearly referring to swordsmanship in this section, although these lessons generally are also applicable to strategy in general, so this could be Way of Strategy.

[38] One *ri* (里) is 2.44 miles (3.9km).

[39] *Ukabi* (written phonetically) – literally "float up".

[40] The word here, *tokudō* (得道), is literally "acquire the Way"; it is a Buddhist term and usually means "become enlightened".

[41] 1667

[42] See "Ground" note 37.

Fire

[1] One *sun* is one tenth of a *shaku* (approximately 30cm/1ft), so this measurement is between 9cm and 15cm (3.5–6in).

[2] Literally "hardened with the six articles" ("tools" [of armour]) *rokugu/rikugu de katamete* (六具でかためて) – the six articles being the helmet, breastplate, shoulder and forearm guards, and thigh and shin plates. The word *gu* (具) is more commonly used to mean "tool", but here that word in English does not quite apply.

[3] The *bushi* wore their two swords at the left side, and if blocked off there it would be very difficult to draw them.

[4] As before, in Japanese this is literally "keeping the right in mind", but since Japanese is traditionally written from right to left and vertically, this has the meaning of "what is written to the right"; that is, previously – the equivalent when writing in English is "above".

[5] The *kamiza* (上座) or "upper seat".

[6] *Mitsu no sen* (三つの先): *sen* (先) means "ahead", "first", or "front tip/end". In the context here, and elsewhere, it is used to mean "the initiative" in strategic action. The first type Musashi gives here is *ken no sen*, with *ken* written phonetically at first, which could have a variety of meanings; later, though, it is written as 懸, which literally means "hang", but is also used in the sense of

"advance" (an attack), and the meaning is also clear from context. The second type, *tai no sen*, is also written phonetically at first but then with 待 (*tai*, "wait"), again making the meaning clear. The last is *tai-tai no sen*, which, although it resembles the second phonetically is written with different *kanji* from the outset: 躰々 (*tai-tai*, the second character indicating duplication), literally meaning "body-body", and here having the sense of "simultaneous".

[7] This is "*zun to*" – there is no exclamation mark (there was no such mark in Japanese at the time); *zun*, however, is an onomatopoeic with the sense of "suddenly and violently", hence the translation "boom!".

[8] 100–125 miles (160–200km).

[9] *Ken wo fumu*: here this is written out all in phonetic *hiragana* characters. Later the word *ken* in the same phrase appears as the *kanji* 劔 ("sword"), but it is possible that initially this was intended to be the *ken* mentioned previously in "The three kinds of initiative" – meaning "advance" or "attack" (懸). Thus this could also be interpreted more abstractly as "stomping down the advance" or "stomping down the attack".

[10] "Four hands" (*yotsude* 四手) is an expression in *sumō* wrestling, referring to a position where both of each wrestler's hands are engaged and neither is able to establish an advantage – that is, a deadlock or impasse. It can also refer to a kind of wrap worn by women in which the four corners of a square cloth are knotted together, but the former meaning is clearly more relevant here.

[11] *Kage wo ugokasu* – the word *kage*, which I have translated as "shadows", here is written in phonetic *hiragana*. Interestingly, there are a number of different possible meanings for this word, two of which are basically opposite: one, usually written with the character 影 or 景, can mean "figure/shape", "light", "shadow", "image" or "reflection", among other things. Another, written with 蔭 or 陰, more specifically means "shade" or "something hidden". In context, the latter seems to be obviously what is meant here (see also "Stifling the form", pages 150–151).

[12] Positions where the sword is partially or entirely obscured from view make it very difficult to anticipate what sort of technique will be used.

[13] "The beat" here indicates a brief, momentary chance to take the victory.

[14] What is translated here as "the form" is also *kage* (see note 11), but in the section title is given with the character 影, indicating something which can be seen (even when used to mean "shadow" it means the positive shape of a shadow, rather than that which cannot be seen because it is in darkness).

[15] 空なる心より: "emptiness-becoming mind-from" – I interpret this to mean "without your intention consciously in mind, and thus without giving away any signal of your impending action."

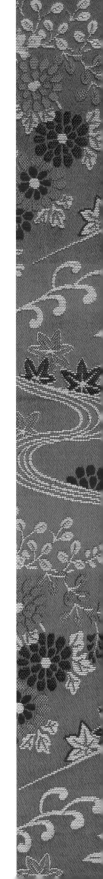

16 This somewhat esoteric concept is similar to the idea of "Striking the opponent in one beat" described in "Water". The implication is that by identifying the enemy's rhythm, you can create your own ("advantageous") rhythm that forestalls him, and strike him when he stops.

17 See note 14.

18 *Muri* (無理) "No principle" – this usually has the sense of something being impossible, so this might also be rendered as "the feeling of attempting the impossible".

19 This tactic is often depicted in films when an army shows itself as a small force to draw its opponents in, then suddenly reveals the true (and usually overwhelming) number of troops, terrifying the enemy and routing them. See also "Mouse's head–horse's neck", pages 169–170.

20 This word is written phonetically as *mabururu,* and could be an earlier form of *mabureru* (塗れる), "to plaster", but given the context I think it more likely that it is an earlier variant of *majireru* (混じれる), meaning "to mix in" or "to become blended".

21 This is given phonetically as *saharu,* an older form of *sawaru,* which has often been interpreted as 触る (*sawaru*) "to touch", but which to me in this context almost certainly means 障る (*sawaru*) "to injure" or "to damage".

22 See also "Understanding collapse", pages 142–143.

23 The word used here is *koe* (聲), which literally just means "voice". However, in the expression *koe wo kakeru,* a phrase Musashi uses later, it means "shout", "cry out" or "call out" (shouts of approval from the audience at *sumō* bouts or kabuki performances are called *kake-goe*), so it is clear from the context in most cases that this sense of "cry" or "shout" is the one in which he is using the word.

24 Alternately, "cutting through intervals". Written in this section phonetically as *magiru,* traditionally this has been treated as a variant of *magireru* (紛れる), meaning "mix together", but I believe this interpretation to be in error; it is both redundant with the earlier explanation of *mabururu* (see "Mixing in" and note 20, above), and it ignores an obviously more pertinent interpretation of *magiru,* which is 間切る ("cutting intervals"), used to describe the approach employed by sailors to cut through the breaks between waves. This latter meaning clearly matches the content of this section.

25 *Tsuzura-ori,* or "bamboo-box folding": that is, in a back-and-forth or zigzag pattern.

26 Some versions have this as "ox's neck"; the old character for "horse" (午) and the character for "cow" or "ox" (牛) are very similar, and can have the same Sinitic reading ("*go*"), which is what is here given in phonetic script in every version of the text. I am mainly using the Hosokawa copy, which gives the "horse" character later, and I follow that here. Although scholarly opinion is not unanimous, most scholars cite that there is no real precedent for a comparison of a mouse/rat to an ox in the literature, and for a warrior like Musashi the horse would have been a more immediately familiar and natural comparison to make.

[27] The image here is of totally unexpected changes in scale, which serve to disorient an opponent.

[28] I believe implicit here is that this is the Way of Strategy, as Musashi is addressing his students (and those who will study his style in the future); since "Fire" is about battle specifically, it is hard to imagine that this is meant to apply to a very broad variety of "Ways".

[29] See note 34, in "Water".

[30] Here again Musashi seems to be criticizing a tendency for the martial arts to become esoteric, something studied in rarified schools for their own sake rather than tested in real battle for their practical application – "more flower than fruit".

Wind

[1] That Way being the *Ni Tō Ichi Ryū* ("Two Swords One Style"). However, as noted previously, Musashi uses two different names for the style at various points in the text: "Two Swords One Style" and "Two Heavens One Style". He also variously refers to the Way of Strategy, which I take to be broader, and inclusive of Musashi's school but not limited to it (Musashi did recognize the values of other schools as well as their weaknesses), and the Way of Warriors (or Way of the Warrior), which is broader still, encompassing everything in the ethos of the warrior class.

[2] All of this from "the good…" to the end of the sentence is one four-character expression: 善悪理非 (*zen-aku-ri-hi*), which is more commonly understood as "good and bad, right and wrong"; I have taken a somewhat more literal interpretation of the latter half: *ri* (理) is "[natural] principle", and *hi* (非) is "not, outside".

[3] *Issun te masari* 一寸手増り: "extending the hand by one *sun*" (3cm/1in).

[4] Common practice when going indoors, particularly as a guest, was to remove the long sword and leave it near the door, wearing only the short sword when seated.

[5] *Tameshigiri* (試し切り) or "test cutting" – to test the quality of a blade, the skill of a swordsman, or both (see also note 5 in "Water"). Its most callous

and horrific form, outlawed by the Edo *bakufu* government in 1602, was *tsujigiri* (辻斬り) – "street-corner killing" – in which some *bushi* endeavoured to test their blades or skill by cutting down random passersby on the road.

⁶ A long pole with a sword – see note 26, scroll of "Ground".

⁷ See "The progression of five standard forms" in "Water", pages 94–98.

⁸ This final exhortation, a type very common in the whole text, does not appear at the end of this particular section in many copies. This may be due to oversight on the part of a transcriber or transcribers at some point or, conversely, it may have been added later in some versions. It does appear in the Hosokawa copy, my main reference, so I have included it here.

⁹ *Shōbu* 勝負 literally means "victory [or] defeat", but it was and is a term often used to mean single combat, or today, more metaphorically, a decisive moment of any kind. *Shōbu no michi* was the idea of single combat as a way of life, adopted by many swordsmen historically, testing their skills against others again and again – not infrequently with the loser winding up dead.

¹⁰ This whole section (starting from "As for the Way…") is also missing from many copies of the text, but it appears in the Hosokawa copy.

¹¹ This is not so clearly elaborated in the text, which only says that this means *kamae ha atte kamae ha naki* – "there is position and [at the same time] there is no position." I have included clarification based on my own experience in a *Ni Ten Ichi Ryū* school.

¹² *Kemari* (蹴鞠), literally "kickball", was a sport played mainly by courtiers, but which had achieved wider popularity in Musashi's time. Played in teams of four to eight players, the objective is to keep the ball (*mari*) aloft using a variety of techniques and without using the hands. The game is a variant of the Chinese game of *cuju* (written with the same characters), which was introduced to Japan in the seventh century CE.

¹³ This is a *kemari* technique, the name of which is recorded in early documents on the sport, but its exact nature is unclear. Musashi writes it phonetically, but in other documents it can be found as 鬢ずり, meaning "scraping the hair of the temples", so it may have been some sort of heading technique, though in that case it would be hard to understand why Musashi would use it with the verb *keru* 蹴る, "to kick".

¹⁴ This is another *kemari* technique, but about this one more is known. Written 負鞠, *ohimari* is a technique in which the *mari* (ball) is kicked high in the air, caught on the back, and bounced up and down there.

¹⁵ The word here is *eru*, which means get/attain/procure/acquire/obtain; it lacks the force of a verb such as "seize".

¹⁶ This is a pun: the word "lacking" or "insufficient" (*busoku*) is written "not-foot" (不足) – the character for "foot" (足) with its Sinitic reading of *soku*

often signifies "sufficiency" (the native Japanese or "Yamato" reading of the same character, *ashi*, has no such meaning). Thus Musashi, after talking about all of these different "feet", then says these are to be considered "not feet".

[17] *Okori*, here written phonetically, is still used in modern *kendō* (written 起こり) to mean "an observable moment when a technique begins". Ideally, one's adversary should not be able to see such a moment, which gives them advance warning that an attack is coming.

[18] *Tobite itsuku kokoro ari* (飛ていつく心有): A word-by-word literal translation would be, "Jumping, being-in-place-attach feeling there-is." Musashi has written earlier about *itsuku* (becoming settled, fixed, or frozen) and how that is to be avoided (see page 100 in "Water"), but here exactly when one is fixed in place is not entirely clear. It is possible Musashi means that while airborne one is "frozen in place", but it seems to me more likely that he means this is the case when one lands.

[19] I am virtually certain that this is describing the kind of bouncing on the balls of the feet that you often see accomplished boxers do.

[20] *Fumi-tsumuru ashi*. This can be seen in many samurai movies: taking a wide stance with the hips lowered, the fighter "creeps" his feet forwards (or in whatever direction). *Fumi* means "stepping" and *tsumu(ru)*, here written phonetically, could be either 積む (る), "pile up, accumulate", or 詰む (る), "squeeze, cram in" (in modern Japanese the final –*ru* is not present).

[21] 100–125 miles (160–200km).

[22] "The Old Pine" is a well-known Noh piece that would have been quickly recognizable to Musashi's audience.

[23] Another Noh piece that would have been familiar in Musashi's day. The title is the name of a town in present-day Hyōgo prefecture.

[24] This last part is "*ma ni ahazu*," (間にあはず) an older form of the modern Japanese expression *ma ni awanai* (間に合わない), which literally means "does not match the interval" and in theory this could be what Musashi intends here, but its idiomatic meaning of "be late, not be in time for something" seems to match the context better.

[25] See note 9 in "Water".

[26] *Kokoro no oyobi-gataki koto* (心のおよびがたき事): "things which do not easily lead the heart/mind".

[27] *Kokoro no hodoku tokoro* (心のほどく所): "places where the heart/mind becomes disentangled/untied".

[28] This may be an allusion to a Zen analogy referring to mountains. The Chinese Zen monk Qingyuan Xingsi/Ch'ing-yüan Hsing-ssu (known in Japanese as Seigen Ishin) said that before he studied Zen, he saw a mountain as just a mountain, and waters as just waters. When he understood Zen

better, he saw that mountains were not mountains, and waters were not waters. But when he became enlightened in Zen, he saw the mountains just as mountains again, and the waters as just waters. In Zen there is a concept known as "beginner's mind", which means seeing things newly and freshly, as if for the first time, without preconceptions. Musashi seems to be implying that in anything if you go deeply enough you arrive at the beginning.

[29] The first time this expression is used. Musashi seems to see many of these expressions as interchangeable, or at least often encompassing overlapping ideas. My sense is that this is a more general Way, along the lines of the meanings with which Musashi uses Way of Strategy or Way of the Warrior.

[30] *Godō-rokudō* (or *–rikudō*) 五道六道. This is a Buddhist term referring to the five worlds of existence: *jigoku* (地獄) "hell", *gaki* (餓鬼) "hungry spirits" [lesser demons], *chikushō* (畜生) "beasts", *ningen* (人間) "humans", and *tenjō* (天上) "heaven". Added to this was sometimes a sixth: that of *ashura* (阿修羅) "protector deities", which originally had been evil demons that fought against the gods in Indian mythology, but later in Buddhism became identified as protectors of the Buddhist teachings. In traditional Buddhist thought, all of these worlds are bad, because they are obstacles to *nirvana* – the release from the cycle of suffering that is death and rebirth. These were/ are also known as the *go/roku akushu* (五/六悪趣) "five/six evil inclinations" or *go/roku akudō* (五/六悪道) "five/six evil ways/paths". It is not entirely clear why Musashi includes this reference. It seems to imply that the warrior's Way is somehow the same as the Buddhist one, and that the same obstacles need to be overcome; that realizing the Way of Strategy is essentially the same thing as a Buddhist enlightenment. It may be, however, that in Musashi's time this was simply a term that had come to mean "obstacles" in general (as many other terms originating in Buddhism took on much more mundane senses). Some have contended that Musashi was sarcastically comparing the shortcomings of other styles to conditions such as "hell", which is possible, but seems unlikely, because "heaven" is also one of the Five/Six Worlds.

Emptiness

[1] See the general introduction.

[2] Here Musashi is clearly drawing a distinction between "strategy" (*heihō* 兵法) and "other martial arts" (*bugei* 武藝); it seems most likely that he is referring to strategy in a more general sense, but it is possible that he is using the more colloquial meaning of "swordsmanship".

[3] *Shin-i futatsu no kokoro* (心意二ツの心). Made up of two characters which

already represent highly abstract ideas, *shin-i* (心意, "heart/spirit/mind – will/meaning/intention") can have a number of interpretations; here Musashi seems to be referring to complementary elements of the psyche, one which should be pure, clear, unmoved/unmoving and "empty", and one which should be forceful and vital. This is related to the *yin–yang* concept, which would have been widely familiar to Musashi's audience.

[4] There is no singular-plural distinction for nouns in Japanese, so this could be translated as "the dual eyes", "the eyes of both" or "both the eyes". However, this abstract idea seems to me to be better presented in parallel with the "twofold heart" previously.

[5] Here more literally "the straight Way" (in other cases Musashi uses a word meaning "true" as opposed to "false"); I have opted for the more abstract phrasing of "true". The latter does also retain the same literal sense of "straight", although less prominently.

[6] *Jitsu no kokoro* (実の心): *jitsu* can also mean "substance" or "fruit", "result", but in this case it stands for the compound *shinjitsu* (真実), meaning truth in the abstract – one's true mind (or heart), and its ability to perceive the correct, unclouded by wrong-headed thinking.

[7] This last section, written as a poem, is not included in the Chikuzen Branch copies of the text, and some scholars believe it was not in the original, but was added later by one of Musashi's students. It is included in the Hosokawa copy, and thus I have included it here. Even if not specifically included by Musashi originally, it is extremely unlikely that a student or follower would have taken it upon himself to add such an invention of his own; it may have been a poem of Musashi's well known among his students and passed down through oral tradition. The sense of the poem really turns on the interpretation of *kokoro* (心) in the final line: *kokoro ha kū nari* 心は空也. While the word can mean variously "mind", "spirit", "central idea", "essence" or "heart", I have chosen the last, as I read this as having a double meaning: both that the heart (mind/spirit) of the *practitioner* attains a state of Emptiness (loss of ego/self-consciousness, and thus oneness with the Way), and that in fact the heart (essence) of *all things* is Emptiness (the illusory nature of permanence falling away to reveal constant change).

Hyōhō Sanjū-go Ka Jō

[1] Here we see a very different style of discourse from the *Go Rin no Sho*, but one that can be found in letters known to be in Musashi's hand.

[2] 手足 *te-ashi* could also be "arms and legs" (*taishō* means "general").

[3] Presumably "this thing" refers to the idea that the mind should be completely fluid and never fixed in one "place".

[4] Literally, "with the mind just as it is" (こころの儘 *kokoro no ma-ma*).

[5] Or "feet" (*ashi*).

[6] "Cause the enemy's mind to move" (敵の心を動かす *teki no kokoro wo ugokasu*).

[7] That is, closing the distance between yourself and the enemy. There is another famous saying in swordsmanship, often attributed to Yagyū Muneyoshi, related to this: "Under crossed swords lies hell, but one more step forwards is heaven" – that is, if you get close enough to your adversary, he cannot strike you with his sword.

[8] Oddly, the explanations for using the two senses of *kage* (陰/影), the negative and the positive, here are reversed from those in the *Go Rin no Sho* (see note 11 in "Fire").

[9] Alternatively, a "great opponent", possibly in status rather than in size.

[10] Most likely the Way of Swordsmanship, but this is possibly meant more broadly in a sense that could be applicable to any given situation.

[11] *Zanshin/hōshin* (残心/放心): The idea of *zanshin*, or "retained/remaining mind", a term commonly used in the Japanese martial arts, is difficult to explain, but refers to sustained attention and the focusing of energy; *hōshin* is the "releasing" of that attention and energy, allowing more freedom.

[12] This explanation is substantially different from the one in *Go Rin no Sho*.

[13] Literally "having neither left nor right hand".

[14] It is unclear why only the left is specified here; it may be a copying error.

[15] The door in the title is apparently a kind that turns on a pivot, like a revolving door, except it doesn't go all the way around (this would be understood not from the title but from the specific word for "hinge" used in the first line). So if you can imagine for example pushing on one side of the door and getting hit by the other side, that is the image.

[16] Literally "three colours" (三色 *san shoku*) – see note 17.

[17] These "three attitudes" are called *jodan* or "upper step" in Japanese. The "raised attitude" refers to the sword(s) being held above the level of the shoulders. The other two "attitudes" are *chudan* ("middle step") and *gedan* ("lower step"). The three "colours" or "ideas" are not made explicit here, but in practice depend on variations in height, which sword is held forwards of the other, and so on.

[18] Literally "ten thousand principles".

[19] 万理一空 This is a four-character phrase of a type widely imported from Chinese literature. Part of this, *banri*, as noted above, means "ten thousand principles" ("ten thousand" is often used to designate "countless" or even

"all"). The other part is "one" and "Emptiness", as explained further in the notes to the "Emptiness" scroll of the *Go Rin no Sho*.

[20] The tone here suddenly returns to the humble form used at the beginning.

[21] If one counts, there appear to be thirty-six rather than thirty-five articles, but it may be that "On myriad Principles, a single Emptiness" is not meant to be considered as one of the "articles".

[22] A calendar of assigning levels of luck to the individual days was imported from China in the fourteenth century, around the end of the Kamakura era in Japan (it is believed to have been extant in China since around the third century). The calendar divides the days into six degrees of auspiciousness, which revolve in a cycle, with five cycles in each month, and the beginning day of each month also revolving. In the second month, the first auspicious day (usually referred to as *tai-an* 大安 but also known as *kichi* 吉, as it is given here) is the fourth, so the date referred to here could be the 4th, the 10th, the 16th, the 22nd or the 28th.

Dokkōdō

[1] The title *Dokkōdō* (独行道) is very ambiguous. Literally "alone/independent" – "go" – way/path"; it could also be "The Way of Going Alone", "Walking the Path Alone", "The Way Gone Alone", "The Way of Going Independently", "The Path Taken Independently" or even "The Way of Self-Reliance". I have therefore opted for an accurate meaning that is slightly more poetic.

[2] The word *monoimi* 物忌み referred to a wide variety of things that had to be avoided in certain situations for purification purposes, from food to colours to numbers to members of the opposite sex. Musashi was probably referring mainly to fasting, but this downplaying of religious practice is consistent with the later admonition about "Buddha and the gods".

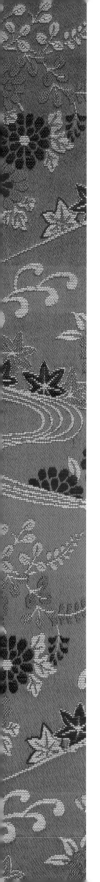

FURTHER READING

SOURCES IN ENGLISH
Carroll, John. *Lightning in the Void.* New York: Printed Matter Press, 2006.

Cleary, Thomas. (trans.) *Code of the Samurai.* North Clarendon, Vermont: Tuttle Publishing, 1999.

Cleary, Thomas. (trans.) *Soul of the Samurai.* North Clarendon, Vermont: Tuttle Publishing, 2005.

De Lange, William. (trans. and ed.) *The Real Musashi: Origins of a Legend – The* Bushū Denraiki. Warren, Connecticut: Floating World Editions, 2009.

De Lange, William. (trans. and ed.) *The Real Musashi: Origins of a Legend II – The* Bukōden. Warren, Connecticut: Floating World Editions, 2011.

Dening, Walter. *Japan in Days of Yore.* London: Griffith, Farran, & Co., 1887. (Reprint, London: Fine Books, 1976.)

Nitobe, Inazo. Bushido*: The Soul of Japan.* Tokyo, New York and London: Kodansha International, 2002.

Takuan, Sōhō. *The Unfettered Mind.* (trans. William Scott Wilson.) Tokyo, New York and London: Kodansha International, 1986.

Tokitsu, Kenji. *Miyamoto Musashi: His Life and Writings.* Boston: Shambhala Publications, 2004.

Wilson, William Scott. *Lone Samurai: The Life of Miyamoto Musashi.* Tokyo, New York and London: Kodansha International, 2004.

Yoshikawa, Eiji. *Musashi.* (trans. Charles S. Terry.) Tokyo, New York and London: Kodansha International, 1981.

SOURCES IN JAPANESE

Imai, Masayuki. *Ni Ten Ichi Ryū seihō.* (*Two Heavens One Style Method.*) Oita, Japan: Imai, 1987.

Miyamoto Musashi (Shinmen, Musashi). *Go rin no sho.* (*Writings on the Five Rings.*) Edited with commentary by Kamata, Shigeo. Tokyo: Kodansha, 1986.

Miyamoto Musashi (Shinmen, Musashi). *Go rin no sho.* (*Writings on the Five Rings.*) Edited with commentary by Kamiko, Tadashi. Tokyo: Tokuma Shoten, 1963.

Miyamoto Musashi (Shinmen, Musashi). *Go rin no sho.* (*Writings on the Five Rings.*) Edited with commentary by Nakamura, Naokatsu. Tokyo: Kodansha, 1970.

Miyamoto Musashi (Shinmen, Musashi). *Go rin no sho.* (*Writings on the Five Rings.*) Edited with commentary by Watanabe, Ichiro. Tokyo: Iwanami Shoten, 1985.

Miyamoto Musashi (Shinmen, Musashi). *Hyōhō go rin no sho.* (*Writings on the Five Rings of Strategy.*) A facsimile of the Hosokawa family scrolls. Tokyo: Kodansha, 1970.

Miyata, Kazuhiro. *Miyamoto Musashi jissen Ni Ten Ichi Ryū hyōhō.* (*Miyamoto Musashi's Real-combat Two Heavens One Style Strategy.*) Tokyo: Bungeisha, 2002.

Yoshida, Seiken. *Ni Tō Ryū wo kataru.* (*Explaining the Two Sword Style.*) Tokyo: Kyozaisha, 1941.

Yoshida, Yutaka. (ed.) *Budō hiden sho.* (*Book of Secret Transmissions on the Martial Way.*) Tokyo: Tokuma Shoten, 1973.

"Miyamoto Musashi" website (in Japanese, 2003)
Harima Musashi Kenkyūkai (Harima Society for the Study of Musashi). www.geocities.jp/themusasi1/index.html

INDEX

ACKNOWLEDGMENTS & PICTURE CREDITS

ACKNOWLEDGMENTS

For the opportunity to do this new translation I owe a great debt of gratitude to my editor, Christopher Westhorp, who somehow tracked me down from the other side of the globe and proposed that I undertake this work, and whose insightful comments and questions were invaluable in producing it in a readable form. I also must again thank Washio Kenshin sensei, my teacher in Musashi's *Ni Ten Ichi Ryū* as well as other martial arts; without his long years of patient instruction it is unlikely that I would have been capable of such an undertaking in the first place. His assistance and clarifications were indispensable in the research for and writing of this book, and his own ceaseless study has been a model of the balance between scholarship and martial skill that the *bushi* aspired to, as well as a constant inspiration to me. I am indebted to the scholars at the Harima Musashi Kenkyūkai (the Harima Society for the Study of Musashi) for making digital versions of virtually every known copy of the *Go Rin no Sho* available as a database, saving me the tremendous amounts of time that otherwise would have been required to find and decipher them all; their commentary was also extremely informative. For providing an ideal environment in which to do a large portion of the work for this book in a relatively short period of time, as well as for a lifetime of support and encouragement, I thank my parents, Donald and Nicole Groff. Finally, I would like to thank my wife Motoko for her patience, understanding and support throughout the whole, very intensive project.

PICTURE CREDITS

The publisher would like to thank the following people, museums, and photographic libraries for permission to reproduce their material. Every care has been taken to trace copyright holders. However, if we have omitted anyone we apologize and will, if informed, make corrections to any future edition.

Key:
(**a**) = above, (**b**) = below

Page 1 Musashi Miyamoto with two *bokken*, *c*.1848, from a series of colour woodblock prints "Fidelity in Revenge" by Utagawa Kuniyoshi (1798–1861), Private Collection; **2** Man in samurai costume, Sanja Matsuri festival, Senso-ji, Asakusa, Travel Pix Collection/awl-images; **4–5** Morning mist, Nara prefecture,

Tomonari Tsuji/amanaimages/Corbis; **6** Miyamoto Musashi, a woodblock print, *c.*1843, by Utagawa Kuniyoshi, Museum of Fine Arts, Boston, Massachusetts/ Bequest of Maxim Karolik/The Bridgeman Art Library; **32** An ink on paper drawing of a bird on a branch by Miyamoto Musashi, Philadelphia Museum of Art/Corbis; **47** Stone lanterns at Kyoto's Adashino nenbutsu-dera temple, Christian Kober/awl-images; **49** An Edo-period ceramic ladle stand from Kyoto, Freer Gallery of Art, Smithsonian Institution, Washington, DC/Gift of Charles Lang Freer/The Bridgeman Art Library; **50** A woodblock print, 1857, of rice planting during a summer shower, from the series "One Hundred Views of Famous Places in Edo" (*Meisho edo hyakkei*), Erich Lessing/akg-images; **55** Two sixfold screens of waterfowl painted in ink and gold dust on paper by Musashi for Hosokawa Tadatoshi, *c.*1640, Eisei-Bunko Museum, Tokyo; **59** A detail of the Nadi Botokesan *buddha* at the Senso-ji, Asakusa, Tokyo, Ron Koeberer/Aurora Open/Corbis; **63** A *kabuki* depiction of an officer of the law, armed with a *naganata*, being overpowered, woodblock print *c.*1830–44, Fitzwilliam Museum, University of Cambridge/The Bridgeman Art Library; **64** A detail of a depiction of the siege of Osaka Castle by Kuroda Nagamasa, Werner Forman Archive/ Corbis; **66–67** A close-up view of the *tsuba* or sword-guard of a 19th-century samurai sword, decorated with auspicious emblems, Private Collection/Corbis; **71** Watercolour of a samurai on horseback, Private Collection/Corbis; **74** A tea plantation in Kanaya, Shizuoka prefecture, Ocean/Corbis; **81** A stone basin with water in a Japanese *chaniwa* garden, Catherine Karnow/Corbis; **83** An 18th-century portrait of Musashi "open on all eight sides", Sakamoto Photo Research Laboratory/Corbis; **87** A *kabuki* actor in a warrior role, *ukiyo-e* print, 19th century, Bibliothèque des Arts Décoratifs Paris/The Art Archive; **90** *Igagoe katakiuchi no zu*, a woodblock print by Utagawa Kuniyoshi, undated, depicting a famous 17th-century vendetta, akg-images; **93** A Japanese helmet with sword collection, Werner Forman Archive; **96–97** An ornate 14th-century sword by the great swordmaker Osafune Morimitsu, © Victoria and Albert Museum, London; **101** Samurai armour style known as *yukinoshita do*, late 16th or early 17th century, Leeds Museums and Art Galleries (City Museum)/The Bridgeman Art Library; **104–105** A triptych depicting the fight between Miyamoto Musashi and Sasaki Kojirō, 1843–47, by Utagawa Yoshitora (active *c.*1836–87), www.Japanesegallery.co.uk; **109** A garden in Kyoto, Japan, B.S.P.I./Corbis; **114** A fight between the elaborately armoured Ichijo Jiro Tadanori and Notonokami Noritsune, woodblock print, *c.*1820, by Shuntei Katsukawa (1770–*c.*1833), IAM/ akg-images; **119** Reeds reflecting in Lake Biwa, Shiga, Honshū, Ocean/Corbis; **121** *Carp Swimming Upwards*, a woodblock print by Katsushika Taito II (active 1810–53), © Victoria and Albert Museum, London; **124** Lotus flower, John Cleare; **131** Ryōbu-style "floating" *torii* gate at Itsukushima, Gavin Hellier/JAI/ Corbis; **137(a)** Musashi's simple iron *tsuba*, Shimada Museum of Art, Kumamoto; **137(b)** An ornate 18th-century *tsuba* with floral symbolism, © Victoria and

Albert Museum, London; **139** *Maisaka Station*, from the series "53 Stations of the Tokaido Road", a woodblock print by Hiroshige (1797–1858), Albright-Knox Art Gallery/Corbis; **144–145** Miyamoto Musashi in the duelling hall, woodblock print, 1855, Asian Art & Archaeology, Inc./Corbis; **146** A wooden Japanese coffer, 16th–17th century, decorated in mother-of-pearl and lacquer, © Victoria and Albert Museum, London; **149** Illuminated lanterns, Kyoto, Jim Holmes/Axiom; **153** A samurai helmet (*kabuto*) with a *menpō* or faceplate, Sylvain Grandadam/Age Fotostock/Photolibrary; **154–155** Illustration of the eruption of the highly active Honshū volcano Asama-yama, Stapleton Collection/Corbis; **161** Lanterns at the Shinto shrine of Kasuga Taisha in Nara, Jeremy Hoare/Axiom; **162** *The Great Wave of Kanagawa*, from "Thirty-six views of Mount Fuji", *c.*1831, a woodblock print by Katsushika Hokusai (1760–1849), Tokyo Fuji Art Museum, Tokyo, Japan/The Bridgeman Art Library; **166–167** Sacred Mount Fuji, Honshū, Datacraft Co Ltd/ Getty Images; **171** A *karesansui* garden at the Rinzai Zen temple Tofuku-ji, Kyoto, Simon Colmer/GAP Photos; **181** A *wakizashi* by Daijo Fujiwara Tadahiro, 1629, Interfoto/akg-images; **184** Detail of a folding screen depicting the siege of Osaka Castle (1615), Kuroda Collection, Japan/Werner Forman Archive; **191** *Shojiro with a sword*, woodblock by Natori Shunsen, 1924, Private Collection/The Bridgeman Art Library; **194–195** A heron reaches for a willow branch, Philip Yabut/Getty Images; **197** A samurai by Utagawa Kuniyoshi, Private Collection/ Scala, Florence; **200** Bird and flower symbols on an Okinawa *kimono*, Seattle Art Museum/Corbis; **203** Sagano bamboo groves in Arashiyama, near Kyoto, the location for many temples belonging to different Zen sects, JTB Photo/SuperStock; **209** *Buzen Province: Miyamoto Musashi on Ganryu Island*, a woodblock print from sheet 17 of the series "Cutout Pictures of the Provinces", 1852, by Hiroshige, Museum of Fine Arts, Boston, Massachusetts/William S. and John T. Spaulding Collection/The Bridgeman Art Library; **212–213** Zen garden, Peter Adams/ Corbis; **217** Scroll fragment depicting the Battle of Rokuhara, Burke Collection, New York/Werner Forman Archive; **222–223** *Musashi*, triptych by Kunichika, 1888, www.Japanesegallery.co.uk; **229** A tree casts a shadow in a Zen garden, Kyoto, Jim Holmes/Axiom; **232** *Four Swallows* by Hiroshige, 1832, Brooklyn Museum/Corbis; **242–243** *Dokkōdō*, Kumamoto Prefectural Museum, a gift of Mr Takeshi Suzuki.

Borders:
Introduction (from *The Yuzen Japanese Paper* © BNN, Inc.); *GO RIN NO SHO* **Ground** (from *Asian Design*, Dover Publications); **Water** (from *20s Kimono*, © BNN, Inc.); **Fire** (from *Asian Design*, Dover Publications); **Wind** (from *20s Kimono*, © BNN, Inc.); **Emptiness** (from *Kimono Patterns*, The Pepin Press); **HYŌHŌ SANJŪ-GO KA JŌ** (from *20s Kimono*, © BNN, Inc.); **DOKKŌDŌ** (from *The Yuzen Japanese Paper*, © BNN, Inc.); **Endnotes** (from *Kimono Patterns*, The Pepin Press).